CLASSIC SERMONS
ON FAMILY
AND HOME

Compiled by
Warren W. Wiersbe

kregel
PUBLICATIONS

Grand Rapids, MI 49501

Classic Sermons on Family and Home, compiled by Warren
W. Wiersbe. Copyright © 1993 by Kregel Publications, a
division of Kregel, Inc., P. O. Box 2607, Grand Rapids,
MI 49501. All rights reserved.

Cover and Book Design: Alan G. Hartman

Library of Congress Cataloging-in-Publication Data

Classic Sermons on family and home / compiled
by Warren W. Wiersbe.
    p.   cm.— (Kregel classic sermons series)
  Includes index.

    1. Family—Religious life—Sermons. 2. Sermons,
America.
I. Wiersbe, Warren W. II. Series.
BV4526.2.C535 1993   248.4—dc20   92-39329
                                        CIP

ISBN 0-8254-4054-8 (pbk.)

          1 2 3 4 5 Printing/Year 97 96 95 94 93

Printed in the United States of America

CONTENTS

SCRIPTURE TEXT INDEX

PREFACE

THE *KREGEL CLASSIC SERMONS SERIES* is an attempt to assemble and publish meaningful sermons from master preachers about significant themes.

These are *sermons*, not essays or chapters taken from books about themes. Not all of these sermons could be called "great," but all of them are *meaningful*. They apply the truths of the Bible to the needs of the human heart which is something that all effective preaching must do.

While some are better known than others, all of the preachers, whose sermons I have selected, had important ministries and were highly respected in their day. The fact that a sermon is included in this volume does not mean that either the compiler or the publisher agrees with or endorses everything that the man did, preached, or wrote. The sermon is here because it has a valued contribution to make.

These are sermons about *significant* themes. The pulpit is no place to play with trivia. The preacher has thirty minutes in which to help mend broken hearts, change defeated lives, and save lost souls; and one can never accomplish this demanding ministry by distributing homiletical tidbits. In these difficult days, we do not need "clever" pulpiteers who discuss the times; we need dedicated ambassadors who will preach the eternities.

The reading of these sermons can enrich your own spiritual life. The studying of them can enrich your own skills as an interpreter and expounder of God's truth. However God uses these sermons in your own life and ministry, my prayer is that His Church around the world will be encouraged and strengthened.

WARREN W. WIERSBE

5

Christ First—For the Home!

Walter A. Maier (1893-1950) was known around the world as the speaker on "The Lutheran Hour," heard over more than a thousand radio stations. Many of his faithful listeners did not realize that this effective communicator was also professor of Old Testament and Semitic Languages at Concordia Seminary in St. Louis. It was said the Maier spent one hour in preparation for each minute that he spoke on the radio. Many of his radio sermons were published in volumes still treasured by those who appreciate good preaching.

This sermon is found in *Peace Through Christ*, published by Concordia Publishing House, St. Louis, in 1940.

Walter A. Maier

1

CHRIST FIRST—FOR THE HOME!

Learn first to show piety at home (1 Timothy 5:4).

AMONG THE MOST distinguished jurists ever to occupy the United States Supreme Court bench was John McLean of Ohio, remembered particularly because of his courageous antislavery ballot in the Dred Scott case. Justice McLean had been indifferent to the claims of Christ during his earlier life; but one day, after hearing a message on the blessed meaning of Jesus' death, he learned to love the Savior. Before that day of his new birth closed, he rushed home, announcing, "I have just found that Jesus died on the cross for me. Let us go to the drawing room and pray together."

Although a group of attorneys waited in that room to consult him, he declared. "I have given myself to Jesus, and now I propose to invite Him to my house." Addressing the lawyers, he continued, "You may do as you please, stay or go; but I want Christ in this home, and now I am to make my first prayer in my own house." They remained, and from that day Justice McLean lived in the positive, unshrinking faith that kept Christ first for his family.

A deep reliance on Jesus' blood-bought mercies always gives the Savior the principal place in the family circle. When the jailer at Philippi, his heart pierced by penetrating sorrow over his sins, cried, as I pray God you have, *What must I do to be saved?*" and then received the pledge of full, free redemption, *"Believe on the Lord Jesus Christ, and thou shalt be saved,"* this new disciple rose from his despair and—so we like to picture the scene—in the first act of his reborn life helped bring his wife, children, relatives, servants to baptism so that Christ would rule over his entire household.

Martin Luther had hardly started the titanic task of restoring the Christian faith when he sought to win the home for Jesus. Not many years after he began writing the magnificent treatises which have provoked the admiration of friend and foe alike, he prepared especially for fathers a short summary of the saving truth so that they could teach their children the way to heaven. He knew that Christ had to be first in the family.

You see, then, that people in various stations of life, when they find themselves saved by grace, want the husband or the wife, their parents and their children to have the same exalted faith that is theirs. Intensely do they long to meet their own in heaven; and to secure these blessings they know that Jesus must reign supreme in their earthly dwelling. As we declare from shore to shore— in the spirit of our message for today—

Christ First—for the Family!

This is no mere personal plea. It is rather the instruction of God Himself (1 Tim. 5:4), where Saint Paul writes: *"Learn first to show piety at home."*

I. Christ First for the Cleansing of the Home!

This appeal is addressed by the Apostle to children bereft of their fathers. In the world of that day, much more than now, a widow could exist only under heavy handicaps; and Saint Paul reminds Christian children in such families that they must *"learn first to show piety at home,"* love their widowed mothers, support them, and in general follow Christ's teachings. No one who understands the emphasis which both the Old and New Testament lay on the blessedness of keeping Christ in our everyday domestic life will take it amiss when we say that today the plea, *"Learn first to show piety at home!"* may be regarded as addressing itself to all children and to all parents, earnestly pleading that in their family life Jesus "reign supreme and reign alone."

Many modern experts on the home, of course, often have no thought whatever of Christ. They are interested in architecture, but they do not realize that one cannot successfully build the permanently happy home without Jesus. Specialists write pretty books about furnishings and interior decorations, but they push aside the soul beauty that Jesus alone can give. Family financiers speak knowingly of expenditures, budgets, and economies, but with how little attention they sometimes regard the price Jesus paid for their soul's redemption! Domestic doctors discuss education as an aid for the better life, and though they may write many commendable prescriptions, we ought to realize that not public instruction in matters of sex but home-training in the spirit of Christ should be our watchword. American houses need roof and wall insulation against zero weather but, more than that, Christ's heart- and soul-protection against the blasts of many destructive theories. Before Federal housing aid, millions in our country should have heaven's family aid.

As long as sin rules unchecked in any home, the forces of evil that many of you know only too well seek to banish peace by promoting selfishness, lust, hatred, and a dozen other vices. Without Christ people often seem to live in a certain kind of harmony; yet be sure of this: if the Savior is not accepted and acknowledged in our earthly homes, we shall never be acknowledged and accepted in heaven.

With the blessings Jesus offers: the complete forgiveness of purple vice and scarlet sin; the free approach to this mercy by grace through faith; the new heart and the right spirit by which temptation's lure may be restrained and fleshly lusts rejected; His constant companionship for guidance, strength, hope; His invitation, *"Come unto Me"*; His assurance, *"Thy sins are forgiven thee"*; His pledge of heaven, *"Because I live, ye shall live also"*; with all these promises, the love of Christ should be eagerly accepted by every soul throughout the world as the most magnificent mercy that even the power and love of heaven combined could grant sinful man. With all the additional blessings the Savior provides for our home relations: love instead of hatred; happiness despite poverty; joy even in sorrow, the greatest wonder of our age is this, that every hovel and palace, kraal and igloo, every basement tenement and pent-house apartment is not marked by the cross of Jesus

Christ! Instead, as the Scriptures testify, *"men loved darkness rather than light."* I hope that you Christ-denying preachers and liberal church officials who may be listening in have finally convinced yourselves in the light of the present debacle that you must silence the twiddle and twaddle about the inborn goodness of man. If you insist on burdening your souls by denying the verdict of God's Word that *"all our righteousnesses are as filthy rags,"* then look at American homes where, with Jesus, we approach heaven as closely as we can on earth, but where without Christ men and women may come nearer to hell, I think, than any other place in this life!

We hear much of "revival" today, and prayers are uttered from coast to coast that the Spirit would mightily restore faith in Christ to the lukewarm and indifferent; to smug, contented churches where, while the souls of men are dying, the chief concern often seems to be: "What will we have now! A chicken or a covered dish supper? A Christmas bazaar or a New Year's card party?" What America needs is repentance, a deep, personal, unreserved sorrow over sin and a clear knowledge of what unforgiven sin means in its misery here on earth and its endless suffering hereafter. And when the text reminds us to show godliness in the home, we realize that our repentance can well begin with the sins violating our family happiness.

Young people, for example, are systematically urged to set aside the divine code of purity and to live after their own lusts. God's command for youth, *"Keep thyself pure!"* and the church's appeal that before marriage young women remain virgins and young men unsullied is laughed to scorn. Premarital chastity is completely set aside by a growing number of young people who pride themselves that they are living full, satisfied lives when in reality they are actually destroying their own prospects of a happy marriage, weighting their souls with sins so treacherous that the last chapter of the Bible, summarizing a hundred similar warnings, excludes from Paradise all those who continually serve the flesh.

Young people usually follow the example of their elders; and in the adult world wedding vows are often willfully broken by the secret affairs of unfaithful husbands and wives who, imagining that they enjoy the zest of life, instead forge fetters of death for the soul. The curse of broken marriage pledges is not only this, that it cuts off the possibility of a family's full joy, often breaks two homes, inflicts misery on the innocent, ruins reputations, frequently spreads social disease, arouses the conscience so that many hardly know one peaceful moment waking or sleeping; but also, a thousand times worse, the terrifying truth— mark this, you who sneer at purity!—that there is no room in heaven for impenitent adulterers.

Other family sins call for wide yet personal repentance when we hear the Apostle's appeal, *"Show piety at home."* Not once but three times in the Bible's first nine chapters Almighty God lays down the divine command for all generations, *"Be fruitful and multiply!"* Yet just as though there never were a Bible, as though God never existed, unnumbered husbands and wives—and, we say it with shame, many even in Christian circles—by actions that speak infinitely louder than any words say, "We will not be fruitful and multiply!" While God's Word joyfully declares, *"Children are an heritage of the Lord,"* too many people believe that babies are a nuisance restricting ambitions and personal pleasure. So tightly does the practice of keeping the family childless clutch America today that financial journals write long articles on the astonishing profits recorded by birth-control industries which every year help prevent hundreds of thousands of children from coming into existence. Now, not the serious physical consequences that may come from this protracted practice, not the moral collapse which follows showing young people how the consequences of personal impurity can be avoided, not the loss which our nation sustains through families willfully kept childless form the most serious charge against the selfish rejection of parenthood. Sins like those of Onan still arouse the displeasure of the holy God!

Men and women nowhere sink to lower levels than in their own Christless homes. You will agree with me if you have ever seen drunken fathers or, worse, drunken mothers stagger home in an alcoholic rage. Their screaming and cursing are too terrible to describe, you will say; but the filth of drunkenness, the bruised and beaten wives, the whimpering children, the pay envelope squandered in the tavern, the loss of work, good name, and usefulness in life—even all this is only a passing annoyance in comparison with the warning of the Almighty, *"They which do such things shall not inherit the kingdom of God."*

And what shall I say of children who, far from showing *"piety at home"* by loving and obeying their parents in the Lord, have time and money for everyone except the father and the mother who gave them life and supported them during their childhood years? One of the most shocking warnings in the entire Scriptures is the biblical picture which shows us a son who despised to obey his parents as a corpse, perhaps an executed criminal, lying unburied as the ravens eat his dead body and the eagles of the air pluck out his dead eyes. Yet that horrifying end is nothing compared with the punishment of his soul!

I speak rather plainly to you; for would you want me to use vague, uncertain language when the welfare of your home and the eternal blessedness of your soul are at stake? If we are outspoken in condemning sins against the family, we can be even more definite in showing the way to hope and happiness for this group. Where, then, you ask, can we find the power to tear out the weeds of wickedness that sometimes flourish particularly in the garden called the Christian home? Are those right who say that we must build the family with new domestic laws! Is it true that particularly the divorce statutes of the nation should be purged of their opposition to God's marriage code? But just as little as men could ever build a barricade to keep the storm-swept ocean off the length of our Pacific and Atlantic coasts, so impossible it is to stop the riptides of human passions by a protective wall of heavy law books.

Are those doctors of home troubles right whose diagnosis of our family sins reveals that we must have more enlightenment? Even worldly wisdom can help to a certain extent; but when education assumes an anti-Christian bias, when it deliberately degenerates into a tirade against God and His Word, it becomes an invisible T.N.T.

that can blast the home's moral and spiritual walls into irreparable ruins. So much of American culture is veering toward practical atheism that thoughtful leaders in Protestant churches are aroused. Many have come to the deliberate conclusion that their groups must follow the practice long ago adopted by my Lutheran Church, the Catholic Church, and the Christian Reformed Church. This removes the child from influences indifferent or hostile to Christ and puts education under the direct control of the churches themselves. Our entire American system for higher education demands a fundamental reshaping to the end that the most essential part of American college and university life must become not head-training but heart-training, not only brain-building but character-building.

Once more, are those right who say that the hope of the American home lies in the overthrow of the family, the program advocated by radical Socialism and atheistic Communism? We hardly need answer this question after the recent tragedies and the horror that has sickened the minds of millions throughout the world, the diabolical campaign to crush Finland and destroy its Lutheranism. It was dastardly enough when the Red bombing planes rained destruction on Finnish homes, set fire to villages, raped and killed the women; but even more repulsive is the whole communistic program for the home that would make the wife common property, the children wards of the state—a proposal born of hell itself as it helps to produce unparalleled numbers of unmarried mothers, a neglected childhood, a riot of divorce, and a devastation by disease unequaled in modern history.

Because all else fails, the cry of this hour must be: Christ first for the family! We put our appeal into this definite plea: If you live as though Jesus had never died for you on the cross, stop in this moment which may help to decide your destiny for a blessed eternity, and pray to God for guidance so that you may have Him as your Savior and the welcome Guest in your home. By His own promise the eternal Christ will bring peace into your soul, help you start a new chapter in your home life, and strengthen you by His power to love good and hate evil. If you are Christ's, let me ask that at this beginning of another church-year, when our hearts are directed toward receiving the Savior, you make pointed resolutions that Christ will be the First in your families.

Young folks often think the counsel of the church and their parents old-fashioned and unsympathetic with youth. Believe me when I tell you that youth has no greater friend than Christ who Himself knew the problems of young manhood and *"was tempted like as we are."* Plan your future home with Him! Avoid every thought of marriage with an unbeliever for only in exceptional cases can a home divided, for Christ and against Him, have any hope of real happiness! Write this down as your determination, "My partner in life must be of the same true faith; we must worship the same Christ!" Plan to build your own home on the Bible, and it will be built, as the Savior Himself promised, on the immovable Rock.

Parents who know that this is the truth, keep your home a sanctuary of the Almighty! Make the family altar the symbol of the Savior's presence! Raise your voices in prayer and hymns! *"Let the Word of Christ dwell in you richly!"* Keep all suggestive pictures from your walls, lustful volumes from your bookshelves, vile magazines from your reading-tables, programs endorsing divorce and triangle relationships off your radios! Make Christ the unseen Guest at every meal! Too many in America believe the bounties we enjoy daily as the rest of the world gazes in astonishment are automatic and can never be taken from us; but a nation even as large and wealthy as ours can be gripped by famine, and we ought to raise our hearts to God every time we are privileged to enjoy our meals. Before Michael Faraday, electrical genius, began his dinner, he prayed with such force that another scientist who visited him recalled, "I am almost ashamed to call his prayer a 'saying of grace.' In the language of Scripture it could be described as the petition of a son into whose heart God had sent the Spirit of His Son and who with absolute trust asks a blessing from his Father." How tragic by contrast is the fact that many in our country begin their meals as the animals do, without a word or thought of gratitude to Him from whom all blessings flow!

II. Christ First for the Blessing of the Home

When Jesus cleanses the home, He also blesses it with the power to meet the requirements of the text, *"Learn first to show piety at home."* Have you ever realized how Jesus brought comfort, strength, and help to the families that received Him, how His mercy in those ancient days carries a meaningful lesson for modern homes? Are you handicapped by want? Are you one of those families that tomorrow will receive apples and cornmeal as the weekly ration? The Savior whose first miracle was performed in a humble dwelling in far-off Cana as He changed water into wine for a Galilean wedding couple can direct the power of His omnipotence to *"supply all your need."* Instead of turning from this Savior, let Jesus prove His love in your home! Resolve: "Christ shall be First in this family!" Show your faith, and He will show you His power! Trust Him completely, and His mercy will provide for you!

Are you afraid you have closed the door on Christ because of your sins or the bad repute you or your children have brought on the family? In this very moment He stands at the entrance to your heart and home, knocking to gain welcome entrance and promising, *"If any man hear My voice and open the door, I will come in to him and will sup with him."* In the days of His flesh His self-righteous and scornful enemies objected, *"This man receiveth sinners and eateth with them"*; in Jericho He entered the house of the notorious publican with the greeting, *"This day is salvation come unto this house."* Believe with all your heart that the same Savior can bring peace and pardon over your threshold!

Are you clutched by religious doubts? Do you question the power of Christ to keep His word? Because some prayers have not been answered immediately and in the way specified, do you declare that Jesus has failed? Instead of protesting, "I am through with the church!" invite Jesus to your home as the disciples did on the Emmaus road when they pleaded, *"Abide with us, for it is toward evening, and the day is far spent,"* and as your soul in penitent and trusting faith sings, "Abide with me, Lord Jesus," your home will be brightened by a radiant faith.

Is sickness the cross imposed on you? Many of your hearts are heavy because for long years you have not known a single day entirely free from pain. Instead of harboring dark, resentful thoughts, exalt Christ as the First in your home, and you will have the assurance that the same Savior who entered His countrymen's homes to lay His healing hands on fevered brows and to remove the pains of palsy can restore your health, if it be for the welfare of your soul, and, if not, strengthen you for greater joy!

Many young women pray that, if it be God's will, they may have a loving husband and children; yet in His wisdom God has not answered; and it may seem that the chance for this happiness dwindles each year. Rather than lapse into bitterness, protesting against what you call the unfairness of life, give Christ the first place in your heart, and as He brought joy into the family circle at Bethany with its two unmarried sisters and its unmarried brother Lazarus, so the blessed Savior can grant you overflowing happiness. He may have spared you unspeakable suffering. He may have far-reaching plans for your usefulness. He can still grant you the blessing of your own home.

If it seems that death has inflicted a wound that can never heal; if your eyes moisten at the sight of an empty chair; if you listen in vain for a voice forever silent and find a loneliness that can hardly be removed, don't raise your voice to accuse God! Don't charge your heavenly Father with cruelty! Ask the Lord Jesus to rule in your home, and the same ever-blessed Redeemer who proved His power by giving life back to a Galilean girl, stopping a funeral procession to restore a deceased son to his widowed mother, approaching a tomb to speak words of resurrection to the moldering remains of His friend—that glorious Christ, who Himself rose from the dead, will banish brooding darkness from your family circle by His promise, *"Because I live, ye shall live also."*

Hear the Apostle's appeal once more: *"Learn first to show piety at home."* Mothers of America, if your club duties, your social obligations, employment and business, even your church-work interfere with the proper care of your children and prevent the necessary supervision of your home, resign from your literary and musical clubs; give up your office job; reduce the time you are spending for church suppers, ladies' aid entertainments and stay with your children, the precious souls whom God has given you for molding! Bring them to Christ and by the Spirit's help keep them with that Savior! Live for your husband and your family!

Fathers of America, whom God has appointed the priests and guardians of the home, whom He wants to be His priests proclaiming the love of Jesus Christ to your own beloved ones, what are you profited if you gain business success, but, without Christ, lose your own soul and see your own children similarly lost? What advantage will there be for them in eternity if you leave your sons and daughters real estate, stocks and bonds, bank accounts, but do not give them the inheritance of Christian faith? If you are too busy for Christ and His church, too busy for prayer and the Bible, may God Almighty bring you to your knees (if necessary, by sickness, loss, reverses, collapse of hopes), so that you will realize how terrifying it is to live without Jesus, to deprive your own children of His love! Remember, you must first *"learn to show piety at home."*

Children of America, help to keep Christ first in your family! Obey your parents gladly and willingly! Learn about Jesus! Recall how He provided for His mother during His last hours on the cross! Pray to Him morning and evening! Ask your parents to have family prayers!

Let all of us, young and old, learned and simple, white and black, yellow and red, wherever we are and whatever our homes may be, resolve, our faced directed toward Christ's coming, that our Savior shall be First in our family, the Guest of our hearts and homes, until we are with Him in the unbroken eternity of His heavenly homeland! God grant it for His sake! Amen.

Manoah's Wife

Joseph Parker (1830-1902) was one of England's most popular preachers. Largely self-educated, Parker had pulpit gifts that soon moved him into leadership among the Congregationalists. He was a fearless and imaginative preacher who attracted both common people and the aristocracy, and he was particularly a "man's preacher." His *People Bible* is a collection of the shorthand reports of the sermons and prayers Parker delivered as he preached through the entire Bible in seven years (1884-91). He pastored the Poultry Church, London, later called The City Temple, from 1869 until his death.

This sermon is taken from *The Ark of God*, published in 1877 in London by S. W. Partridge and Co.

Joseph Parker

2

MANOAH'S WIFE

But his wife said unto him, If the Lord were pleased to kill us, he would not have received a burnt offering and a meat offering at our hands, neither would he have showed us all these things, nor would as at this time have told us such things as these (Judges 13:23).

THIS IS PART of a family scene. It is quoted from a conversation which took place between husband and wife. I propose to treat the incident in a familiar manner, as showing us some aspects of family life, some methods of reading Divine Providence, and some sources of consolation amid the distractions and mysteries of the present world.

We shall look at it as showing some aspects of family life. Here is the head of the house in gloom. Is he not always more or less in gloom, this same head of the house all the world over? Who ever knew a head of the house that was not more or less low-spirited, worried by a hundred anxieties, tormented by sudden fear? Perhaps naturally so: after all he *is* the head of the house; and probably the lightning conductor, being higher than any other part of the building, may have experience of thunderstorms and lightning discharges that lower parts of the structure know nothing about. As the head of the house you are in the marketplace, you see things in their roughest aspects, you have to bear many a thing that you cannot explain to strangers, and there is an under-current in your consciousness which perhaps your truest friend has never seen, or seeing, appreciated; and therefore when I hear the head of the house complaining in tones that have no music in them, how know I but that the poor man has been undergoing vexations and distresses that he does not feel at liberty to explain? At any rate Manoah took this view of the angel's visit: "We have seen God: no man can see God and live—we shall surely die."

19

Comfort and Cunning

Here we have a wife comforting her husband. Like a true woman, she let Manoah have his groan out. There is a beautiful cunning in love. It does not break in upon a sentence at a semicolon. It lets the groan get right out, and then it offers its gentle consolation. If we had heard Manoah alone, we should have said, A terrible thunderstorm has burst upon this house, and God has come down upon it with awful vengeance; and not until we heard his wife's statement of the case would we have any clear idea of the reality of the circumstances. You complain of this word *but*; when a statement is made to you and it proceeds fluently and satisfactorily, the speaker says *but*, and you say, "Aye, there it is again." We sometimes abuse this *but*; it sometimes, however, introduces all the light and all the music and is found to be the key, long lost, of the gate which had impeded our progress. But his wife said unto him—*but* a certain Samaritan came that way. Therefore remember that help sometimes comes after words that seem only to promise some greater distress.

Be the complement of each other. The husband does not know all the case. Perhaps the wife would read the case a little too hopefully. You must hear both the statements, put them both together, and draw your conclusions from the twofold statement. People are the complement of each other. Woe to that man who thinks he combines all populations and all personalities in himself. That must be a miserable man who thinks he is the only man in the world. You would get more help from other people if you expected more, if you invited more, if you put yourself in circumstances that would justify the offering of more. There is not a poor creature in the world who cannot fill up the drop that is wanting to complete the fullness of some other creature's joy.

You would not be half the man that you are except for your wife, and yet you never say "Thank you" with any degree of heartiness or sincerity. You listen to her suggestions with a half contempt as if she did not know what she was talking about, and then you go and work out her idea and get the profit of it, and say what a clever man of business you are. That is not honest, it is not just—"Thou shalt not steal."

Candor and Confidence

Here we have a husband and wife talking over a difficult case. Is not that a rare thing in these days of rush and tumult and noise when a man never sees his little children, his very little ones, except in bed? He leaves home so early in the morning and gets back so late at night that he never sees his little ones but in slumber. Is it not now a rare thing for a husband and wife to sit down and talk a difficulty over in all its bearings? Have I not known in the course of my pastoral experience a wife wronged because of the husband failing to show proper confidence? The man has been in difficulties, wherever he has gone he has been pursued by a haunting dread, and he has suffered all this alone; whereas if he had but stated the case with all frankness and loving candor, who knows but that his wife might have said some word which might have been as a key to the lock and as a solution of the hard and vexatious problem?

You will always find it an inexpressible comfort to take your husband or wife, as the case may be, into your confidence and talk any difficulty right through, keeping back no part of the case. "It soothes poor misery hearkening to her tale." If we lived in more domestic confidence, our houses would be homes, our homes would be churches, and those churches would be in the very vicinity of heaven.

Let us now look at the incident as showing some methods of reading Divine Providence. There we have the timid and distrustful method. Manoah looks at the case, reads it, spells where he cannot read plainly, and then, looking up from his book, he says to his wife, "There is bad news for you: God is about to destroy us." There are these same timid and doubtful readers of Providence in society today. There are some men who never see the sky in its mid-day beauty, who never see summer in July at all, who really have never one day's true elevation of soul. I do not blame such people altogether.

We are fearfully and wonderfully made. We cannot all read with equal facility and see with equal distinctness. There are causes or sub-causes, intermediate secondary influences arising from physical constitution and other circumstances over which we have no control, which trouble our vision even of God Himself. I put in, therefore, a word wherever I can for those who are not constituted hopefully, who have not been gifted with a sanguine temperament.

There are men amongst us whose life is a continual pain. It is possible so to read God's ways among men as to bring upon ourselves great distress. Is a man, therefore, to exclaim, "This is a punishment sent from heaven for some inscrutable reason, and I must endure it as well as I can; I shall never see the sky when not a cloud bedims its dome"? No, you are to struggle against this, you are to believe other people; that is to say, you are to live in other people's lives, to get out of other people the piece that is wanting in your life. You are not to put ashes upon your head and say, "There is nothing in the universe that I do not see." You are to call little children and to say, "What do you see?" and young men and say, "How does life look from your point of view?" and you are to live in other people.

We are to walk by faith and not by sight; we are debtors both to the Jew and to the Greek; and we must get from one another a complete statement of the reality of God's way among the children of men. This is the inductive and hopeful method of reading Divine Providence. Some cynical people who have no license, and therefore ought to be arrested as metaphysical felons, say that women have no logic. And that sentence sounds as if really it ought to be true. It is so pat. It is one of those little weapons that a man can pick up and use as if he had always had it.

I think that Manoah's wife was in very deed learned in what we call the inductive method of reasoning for she stated her case with wonderful simplicity and clearness. "If the Lord were pleased to kill us, he would not have received a burnt offering and a meat offering at our hands, neither would he have showed us all these things, nor would as at this time have told us such things as these."

That is logic! That is the inductive method!—the method, namely, of putting things together and drawing a conclusion from the aggregate.

Looking on the Bright Side

Thank God if you have a wife who can talk like that. Why, if they had both been gloomy parties, what a house it would have been! They need never have taken the shutters down, and summer might have ignored their existence. But Manoah's wife was of a hopeful turn of mind. She had the eye which sees flecks of blue in the darkest skies. She had the ear which hears the softest goings of the Eternal. She was an interpreter of the Divine thought. Oh, to have such an interpreter in every house, to have such an interpreter in every pulpit, to have such a companion on the highway of venture and enterprise! This is the eye that sees further than the dull eye of criticism can ever see, that sees God's heart, that reads meanings that seem to be written afar. Have we this method of reading Divine Providence? I call it the appreciative and thankful method. Why, some of us can take up our load and say, "Only this!" and say it in a tone that means practical blasphemy; others can take up a crust and say, "Praise God from whom all blessings flow! This is God's gift. He cannot mean me to die, or He would not have put this into my hand." A litany in one sentence, worthy to find its place amid the hallelujahs and blessings of the better world.

Who was it that said, "When I look at those who are higher than I am, I am tempted toward discontent, but when I go out among the poor and compare their condition with my own, my heart overflows with loving thankfulness"? How dare we complain, the worst, the poorest in this house! Taking the average of us—and a low average—what man, what woman is there here who ought not to join in heartfelt praise to Almighty God for mercies innumerable as the moments, delicate as the light, present as the living air round about one's poor life! Manoah droops, pines, dies; his wife goes out, gathers the flowers in the Lord's garden, brings them back to him and says, "Manoah, be a man; would God have given us these things if He meant to kill us?" And poor Manoah lifts up his drooping face to the light. Put together your mercies, look at them as a whole and say, Can this mean death, or does it mean life? and I know what the glad answer will be.

Count Your Blessings

There are some sources of consolation amid the distractions and mysteries of the present world. Every life has some blessings. I charge it upon you at this season of the year to reckon up your blessings. Men eagerly count up their misfortunes and trials, but how few remember their mercies! One man says, I have no wealth. No, but look what a pair of shoulders you have! Another man says, I have but feeble health. True, but look what investments you have! Another voice says, I am disposed to be fearful and dispirited. But look what a wife you have! Every life has some blessing, and we must find what that blessing or those blessings are. We must put them together and reason from the goodness toward the glory of God. Amid these blessings religious privileges are sure signs of the Divine favor. We have religious privileges: we can go into the sanctuary; we can take counsel together; we can kneel side by side in prayer; we can go to the very best sources for religious instruction and religious comfort. Does God mean to kill when He has given us such proofs of favor as these? Does He mean to kill us when He has sent the minister of the covenant to tell us glad tidings of great joy?

Let us find in religious blessings proof that God means no evil to us. We will persist in looking at a distress till it seems to be the only thing in our life. We need to put two and two together. Do not be losing yourselves in the midst of details that have apparently no connection. Gather up your life until it becomes shaped into meaning, and then when you have seen things in their proper relationships, pronounce calmly upon the ways of God toward you. Let us put away religious melancholy. Many people have come to me saying, "I fear I have committed the unpardonable sin; I seem to have offended God forever, and put Him far away from me, so that I can never see His face again." Would you have any anxiety about the thing if He were clean gone forever and had drawn the skirts of His garments after Him so as to leave you but the blackness of darkness? By the very fact of your concern understand that God has not purposed to kill you. Cry mightily for Him; say, "Oh that I knew where I might find Him!" "Why standest Thou afar off, O God?" And if you cry so, He will surely come again, saying, "For a small moment have I forsaken thee, that with everlasting mercy I might gather thee."

Let us learn from this family scene that great joys often succeed great fears. Manoah said, The Lord intends to kill us; his wife said, Not so, or He would not have received a burnt offering at our hands. And behold Samson was born, a judge of Israel, an avenger of mighty wrongs. Is it ever so dark as just before the dawn? Are you not witnesses that a great darkness always precedes a great light—that some peculiar misery comes to prepare the way for some unusual joy? If we could only lay hold of life in this way, and read it, not with unreasonable expectation of deliverance and joy, but with hopefulness, we should never become old, desiccated, or tuneless—to the last we should wear like old silver, to the very last there would be in us a light above the brightness of the sun. Let us read the goodness of God in others. Many a time I have been recovered from practical atheism by reading other people's experience. When things seem to have been going wrong with myself, I have looked over into my neighbor's garden and seen his flowers, and my heart has been cheered by the vision.

Words for Women

Oh, woman, talk of your mission! Here is your mission described and exemplified in the case of the wife of Manoah. What do you want with your School Board and platform experiences and those mysterious abstractions which you call your *rights*? Here is your field of operation. Cheer those who are dispirited, read the Word of God in its spirit to those who can only read its cold meager letter, and the strongest of us will bless you for your gentle ministry.

Did not Paul write to the Church at Rome saying, "Greet Priscilla and Aquila," putting the wife's name first, and that in no mere spirit of courtesy, but probably in recognition of her supreme influence in spiritual direction and consolation? Who was it in the days of Scottish persecution? Was it not Helen Stirk—a braver Helen than the fiend Macgregor—who said to her husband as they were carried forth both to be executed, "Husband, rejoice, for we have lived together many joyful days; but this day wherein we die together ought to be most joyful to us both, because we must have joy forever; therefore I will not bid you good night, for we shall suddenly meet within the kingdom of heaven"?

Who was it when Whitefield was mobbed and threatened, and when even he was about to give way—who was it but his wife who took hold of his robe and said, "George, play the man for your God"? Oh, woman, talk of your rights, and your sphere, and your having nothing to do! We should die without you. The man is fit for murders, stratagems, and spoils who is not a worshiper of woman—a worshiper of his mother, of his sister, of his wife, of the ideal woman. Have a sphere of labor at home, go into sick chambers and speak as only a woman can speak. Counsel your sons as if you were not dictating to them. Read Providence to your husband in an incidental manner as if you were not reproaching him for his dullness but simply hinting that you had seen unexpected light.

Women have always said the finest things that have ever been said in the Bible. Why it was a woman that—I speak it with reverence—outwitted the Lord Himself. He said "No" to her request. And He was not accustomed to say that word, it fell awkwardly from His dear lips. "I am not sent but unto the lost sheep of the house of Israel. It is not meet to take the children's bread and cast it unto dogs." But the woman outwitted Him! There was not a Scribe or Pharisee who would not have been silenced, but she said, "Truth, Lord: yet the dogs eat the crumbs which fall from their master's table." And He instantly yielded Himself as a willing prisoner of love.

The finest things that have ever been spoken have been spoken from the heart. The brain may write down its list, and a very fine list too but very cold, and I will undertake to write sentences from the heart which for wit, sparkle, richness, and divinity will cause the brain to double up its list and slink off.

A Mother's Reward—Jochebed

Clovis Gillham Chappell (1882-1972) was one of American Methodism's best-known and most effective preachers. He pastored churches in Washington, DC; Dallas and Houston, Texas; Memphis, Tennessee; and Birmingham, Alabama; and his pulpit ministry drew great crowds. He was especially known for his biographical sermons that made biblical characters live and speak to our modern day. He published about thirty volumes of sermons.

This message was taken from *Sermons on Biblical Characters*, published in New York in 1930 by Richard R. Smith, Inc.

Clovis Gillham Chappell

3

A MOTHER'S REWARD—JOCHEBED

Exodus 2:9

"TAKE THIS CHILD away and nurse him for me and I will give thee thy wages." This text refers to one of the big events of human history. This is one of the most stupendous happenings that was ever recorded. I doubt if there was ever a battle fought that was so far reaching in its influence. I doubt if all the fifteen decisive battles of the world taken together were of greater importance than this event that took place here on the banks of the Nile.

It is a simple story. An Egyptian princess, with her attendants, has come to the riverside for a bath. To her amazement she discovers a strange vessel lying at anchor upon the waters of the river. Her curiosity is aroused. When the vessel is brought to land, its cargo is discovered. And what a cargo it is. It is so wonderful, it is so amazingly great that we marvel that any ship should be large enough to hold it. We are amazed that any sea should be vast enough to float such a vessel.

What was this cargo? It was a baby, a baby boy. He is waving dimpled hands and kicking chubby feet, and he is crying. And the vessel upon which he sails becomes a battleship. He at once begins to lay siege to the heart of the princess. He pelts her with his tears. He pierces her through and through with his winsome weakness. He cannonades her with his lovely helplessness till she capitulates and gathers him in her arms. And this princess is no wicked woman. I am sure of that. She had a mother heart. I think I can hear her across the centuries talking to this little waif. She hugs him close. "Yes, yes," she said. "You shall be my baby. The big, old soldiers shan't have you. They shan't kill mother's little boy." And she loved him as her own.

Now, two bright eyes had been witnessing this wonderful scene. Hidden nearby was a little girl who watched all that happened. And when she saw the princess take her little baby brother to her heart, she understood. She felt sure at once that the baby was safe. And a glad and daring thought took possession of her, and she hurried from her place of hiding and approached the princess. And this is her word, "My lady, may I get a nurse for your baby?"

And the princess did not despise the little girl. I feel perfectly confident that the Spirit of God was moving upon the heart of this princess. She listened to the child and accepted her services. And I can see that little girl as with flying feet she hurries to her mother with the good news. "Mother, they have found Little Brother, but they are not going to kill him. The Princess found him and I told her that I would get somebody to nurse him for her. Come, and we may have him for our own again."

A Death Sentence Rescinded

Now, I take it that it was an important event when the Princess decided that the child was to live. The death sentence had been pronounced against every son of the Hebrews. But an even more important event took place when the Princess decided who should be the baby's nurse. When she decided who should have the training of the child, then she decided what the child was to be. Suppose, for instance, she had determined to train him herself, she would have made him like herself. Moses would have become a heathen in spite of the blood in his veins. He was destined to be a genius, but his genius might have been very far from being the helpful something that it was. Wrongly trained it might have been as brilliant as the lightning's flash, but also as destructive.

But this woman chose, all unwittingly, it is true, to give her baby to be nursed by his own mother. And this Jewish woman was not a heathen. She was a faithful servant of the Lord. I can see her as she hurries down to the banks of the Nile. And as she goes there's a wonderful light in her eyes. And her lips are moving, and she is saying, "Blessed be the God of Abraham and Isaac and of Israel, who has heard the prayer of His servant and who has granted the desire of her heart."

And I love to look again upon this scene. The Egyptian princess is handing over the precious little bundle of immortality into the arms of a Jewish slave. And that Jewish slave is hugging her own child to her hungry heart. And the princess is talking to her proudly, haughtily, as becomes her rank, "Take this child away and nurse him for me and I will give thee thy wages." And away goes this mother, the happiest mother, I think, in all the world.

Now, had you met this mother with her child so wonderfully restored to her and had asked her whose was the child and for whom she was nursing it, I wonder what she would have said. I know what the attendants of the princess thought. I know what they would have said. They would have said that she was nursing the child for the Princess. They would have said that the Princess was her employer. They would have said that Moses was the Princess's baby.

But this mother never thought of it in any such way. She laughed in the secret depths of her heart at the idea of her being employed by the Princess. Who was her employer? I know what she thought. She believed that God was. She had a pious fancy that God was speaking through the lips of that Princess and that He was saying, "Take the child and nurse him for me and I will give thee thy wages." She thought her child was God's child. Therefore, she believed that it was to God, and not to the Egyptian Princess, that she was to account at the last for the way in which she trained and played the mother's part by her boy.

Yes, I feel confident that this mother believed that she was His minister. She believed that she had been chosen for the task that was now engaging her. And she was right in her belief. When God, who had great plans for Moses, sought for someone who was to make it possible for Him to realize His plans, whom did He choose? To whom did He commit this precious treasure, from whose life such infinite blessings should come to the world? He did not commit him to a heathen. He did not commit him to a mere hired servant. He committed him to his mother. When God wants to train a child for the achieving of the best and the highest in life, He sends him to school to a godly mother.

An Immortal Mother

Now, when God chose the mother of Moses for his nurse and his teacher, He made a wise choice. The choice was wise, in the first place, because this mother of Moses was eager for her task. She was a willing mother. Whatever glad days may have come in her life history, I am sure no gladder time ever came than that time when she realized that to her was going to be given the matchless privilege of mothering her own child. I know there are some mothers who do not agree with her. I know there are some that look upon the responsibilities of motherhood as building a kind of prison, but not so this immortal mother. She looked upon her duty as her highest privilege. She entered upon her task with an eagerness born of a quenchless love.

A Woman of Faith

The choice was fortunate, in the second place, because she was a woman of faith. In the letter to the Hebrews we read that Moses was hidden by faith. Both the father and the mother of Moses were pious people. They were people of consecration, of devotion to God, of faith in God. It is true they were slaves. It is true they had a poor chance. It is true they lived in a dark day when the light was dim, but they lived up to their light. And their home was a pious home, and its breath was sweet and fragrant with the breath of prayer.

And I have little hope for the rearing of a great Christian leader in any other type of home. I have no hope of rearing a new and better civilization in any other type of home. Our national life is discordant and hate-torn today. We are living in a time of intense bitterness and selfishness and sordid greed. But what civilization is today, the home life of yesterday has made it. And what civilization will be tomorrow, the home life of today will make it. If we do not have Christian homes, believe me, we will never have a Christian civilization.

"I know Abraham," God said, "that he will command his children and his household after him." And there are two remarkable assertions made of Abraham in this text. First, He said, "I know that Abraham will command; I know Abraham will control his own household. I know that Abraham will control his children." And God considered that as highly important. Of course, we are too wise to agree with Him today. We believe it best to let our children run wild and do largely as they please. We believe that Solomon was an old fogy when he spoke of "sparing the rod and spoiling the child." And I am not here to tell you just how you are to control your child. But what I do say is that you cannot commit a greater blunder than to fail to control it. A child is better unborn than untrained.

Then God said of Abraham next, not only that he would command his children and his household, but that he would command them after him. He would not only exercise the right kind of authority, but he would exert the right kind of influence. He would set the right kind of example. He knew that Abraham would be in some measure what he desired his children to be, that by authority and by right living he would Christianize his own home.

And so when God wanted to raise up a man Moses who was to remake the world, He put him in a pious home. He gave him a godly father and mother. And the dominant influence in the life of Moses was his mother. No woman ever did a greater work. But it was a work that she accomplished not because of her high social standing. Nor was it accomplished because of her great culture. It was accomplished because of her great faith.

And while I am not in any sense a pessimist, I cannot but tremble in some measure for the future because of the decay of home religion. And this decay, while traceable in some measure to the madness for money and pleasure among men, is traceable even more to this same madness among women. The woman of today is in a state of transition. She has not yet fully found herself. There has come to her a new sense of freedom, and this freedom has not made her better. She has become in considerable measure an imitator of man. And sad to say, she imitates his vices instead of his virtues. She often patterns after what is worst in him instead of what is best.

I am told that in the Woman's Club of this city the handsomest room in the building is the smoking room. Now, a woman has a right to smoke. Who says that she has not? A woman has a right to swear, and that right she is exercising with growing frequency. I am not going to deny her right to do that. But what I do say is this, that I have absolutely no hope for the rearing of a right generation at the hands of a flippant cigarette-smoking mother. The child of such a mother is, in my candid opinion, half damned in its birth. Remember, the mother of Moses was a pious mother. If she had not been I am persuaded that the Moses who has been one of the supreme makers of history might never have been known.

Now, what was this woman's task? Hear it. I take these words as embodying not the will of the princess, but the will of God, "Take this child and nurse him for me and I will give thee thy wages." This mother was not to govern the world. She was not to lecture in the interest of suffrage. I have nothing to say against the woman who does so. She was not to be the center of a social set. She was not to turn her child over to some servant woman while she went gadding about to every sort of club. She had just one supreme job. She had one highest and holiest of all tasks. It was for that cause that she came into the world. She was to train her child for God. And whoever we are and whatever may be our abilities, we can have no higher task than this. The training of a child today is the biggest big job under the stars. He is the center of all our hopes and possibilities.

Did you ever read the story of the "Little Palace Beautiful"? In the Little Palace Beautiful there are four rooms. The first is a room called Fancy. In this room looking out toward the south sleeps a little child, a beautiful baby. It is the Child-that-Never-Was. It was longed for, hoped for, dreamed of, but it never came. In the west room looking out toward the sunset, the room called Memory, is the Child-that-Was. Here sleeps the little fellow that came and stayed just long enough to gather up all our heart's love and then he went away. In the room toward the north, the room of Experience, is the Child-that-Is. He is the little fellow who now plays in your home and in your Sunday School class. And in the room looking out toward the sunrise, the room called Hope, is the Child-that-Is-to-Be.

Now, we are interested in all four of these children, but our interest in the four is to be expressed in our care for just one, and that is the Child-that-Is. We think tenderly of the Child-that-Never-Was. We think sadly of the Child-that-Was. But we bring the love that we might have given and did give, to lavish it upon the Child-that-Is. We think hopefully of the Child-that-Is-to-Be, but we realize that all his possibilities are locked in the Child-that-Is. And so the world's future salvation is in our cradles, in our homes, and in our nurseries today. To train our children for God is the highest of all high tasks.

A Mother's Rewards

And notice that this woman was to receive wages for her work. What were her wages? I suppose the princess sent down a little coin at the end of each week, but do you think that is all the pay that this mother got? I feel confident that she never counted this as pay at all. But she received her reward, she received her wages. And they were wages that were rich in worth beyond all our fondest dreams. First, there was given unto her the fine privilege of loving. And Paul, who knew what was priceless, Paul, who knew what was of supreme value, said that love was the soul's finest treasure. And he meant not the privilege of being loved, as fine as that is, but the higher privilege of loving. And it has been given by the grace of God to the mothers of men to be the world's greatest lovers.

> If I were hanged on the highest hill,
> Mother o' mine, O mother o' mine!
> I know whose love would follow me still,
> Mother o' mine, O mother o' mine!

> If I were drowned in the deepest sea,
> Mother o' mine, O mother o' mine!
> I know whose tears would come down to me,
> Mother o' mine, O mother o' mine!
>
> If I were damned of body and soul,
> I know whose prayers would make me whole,
> Mother o' mine, O mother o' mine!

To her was given, in the second place, the fine reward of self-sacrifice. She had the privilege of giving. She had the privilege of offering her life a willing sacrifice upon the altar of her home. It is blessed to receive, but it is more blessed to give. And the rewards of motherhood are the highest rewards because she is the most godlike giver that this world knows.

Then, she was rewarded, in the third place, by the making of a great life. She became the mother of a good man. Her faith became his faith. "By faith Moses was hidden." That was by his mother's faith. But in the next verse we read this, "By faith Moses, when he was come to years, refused to be called the son of Pharaoh's daughter." That was by his own faith. Where did he get that rare jewel? He got it from the training of his mother. He saw it in her life. It looked out from her eyes. It spoke through her lips. He drank it in as he lay in her arms.

"When I call to remembrance the unfeigned faith that is in thee, which dwelt first in thy grandmother Lois and in thy mother Eunice, and I am persuaded is in thee also." Oh, if you are here a man of faith, a woman of faith, the chances are you secured that precious treasure at the hands of a God-loving and God-trusting mother.

So this despised slave woman, this mother has this to her credit, that she mothered and trained one of the greatest men who ever set foot on this earth. She took a little boy named Moses to her heart and trained him for God. She had him for a little while. Then he went away to the big University. But he stood true. She speaks to him as she holds him close in the twilight. She says, "Laddie, do not forget how God has watched over you. One day when death was suspended above your baby head by a thread, one day when your life was frailer than a gossamer thread, I took a little basket and lined it with pitch, and also with faith and with prayer. And I put you afloat, and God preserved you and sent you back into these arms. And I carried you and cared for you. And now when you are grown you won't forget. You won't prove disloyal to your mother and you won't forget your mother's God."

The Mother of a Man

And Moses did not forget. And one day the little laddie who had once been carried about in the arms of a slave mother was a big broad-shouldered man. And he had a big broad-shouldered faith, and he trusted in a big broad-shouldered God. And in the strength of that faith and in the might of that God, he lifted an enslaved people in his arms and carried them clean across the wilderness. And he made possible an Isaiah and a Jeremiah and a David. And he became the blesser and enricher of all the nations of the earth. And this mother, whose name is not well known in the annals of men, but whose name is known in heaven today, had the rich reward of knowing that she mothered a man who fathered a nation and blessed a world.

Oh, it is a blessed reward, the reward of success in the high enterprise of motherhood. I know of no joy that can come to a father's or a mother's heart that is comparable to the joy that their own children can give them. I have seen sweet-faced mothers look upon their children when there was enough joy in those faces to have raised the temperature of heaven.

But while it is true that none can bring us so much joy, it is also true that none can so utterly break our hearts. To see disease take our children in hand and wreck their bodies is painful, but it is as joy in comparison to seeing sin steal the moral rose from their cheek and the sparkle of innocence and purity from their eyes. But the deepest of all damning griefs is that grief that comes to us when we realize that we failed and that their ruin is due to sin and unfaithfulness in ourselves.

Do you hear the wild outcry from that broken-hearted king named David? There he stands upon the wall and looks away across the wistful plain. A lone runner is coming. He knows he is a messenger from the battlefield. "Good tidings," he shouts. But the king has no ear for good tidings. His one question is this, "Is the young man Absalom safe?" And the runner does not rightly answer his question. Then the second messenger comes with the news of his son's death. And there is no more pathetic cry in literature than that that breaks from the lips of this pathetic king. "O my son Absalom, O Absalom, my son, my son!" He is sobbing over his lost boy. But there is an added pang to his grief. It is the awful pang that comes from the torturing fear that he himself is in large measure responsible for the loss of his boy. And there is no more bitter agony than that.

Oh, men and women, let us who are fathers and mothers spare ourselves David's terrible agony. Let us spare our children Absalom's tragic ruin. Let us give ourselves the joys of this old time mother. While our children are about us, may we hear the very voice of God speaking to us on their behalf, saying: "Take this child and train it for me and I will give thee thy wages." And wages we shall receive just as surely as did this mother of Moses. We will be privileged to love, to give, to bless. And God Himself can give no richer reward than that.

The Spiritual Recovery of the Home

George W. Truett (1867-1944) was perhaps the best-known Southern Baptist preacher of his day. He pastored the First Baptist Church of Dallas, Texas, from 1897 until his death and saw it grow both in size and influence. Active in denominational ministry, Truett served as President of the Southern Baptist Convention and for five years was President of the Baptist World Alliance; but he was known primarily as a gifted preacher and evangelist. Nearly a dozen books of his sermons were published.

This sermon was taken from *On Eagle Wings*, published in 1953 by W. B. Eerdmans and reprinted in 1973 by Baker Book House.

George W. Truett

4

THE SPIRITUAL RECOVERY OF THE HOME

Genesis 35:2,3

THE SUBJECT FOR our meditation together today is the spiritual recovery of the home. The subject is suggested for us by these words in the thirty-fifth chapter of Genesis:

> Then Jacob said unto his household, put away the strange gods that are among you and be clean and change your garments and let us arise and go up to Bethel and I will make there an altar to God who answered me in the day of my distress and was with me in the way which I went.

The first institution that God fashioned for the good of human society was the home. Human society is founded to a remarkable degree on the home. The orderly development of society follows upon the orderly development of the home. The greatness of any land depends upon its homes. No nation can rise any higher than its home-life. One of the most beautiful and impressive pictures in all literature, outside the Holy Bible, is Bobby Burn's poem, "The Cotter's Saturday Night." Every father and mother should read it again and again, as it portrays home life anchored to God and bowing obediently to His will. The wise and worthy care of the home is a matter of eternal moment. Well does one of the large classes for women in the Sunday School of this church have for its motto these words: "The Home for Christ."

We are called here to a matter far more important than the secular matters about us to which we give much serious thought and effort. Here is a matter more important than business, important as that is; a matter far more important than statecraft, important as that is; a matter of more importance than our vast system of public education, important as that is. The care of the home, the wise and worthy care of the home goes before any of the important causes I have named. Civilization to a remarkable degree is dependent upon the home. Church and state are both vitally concerned about the home-life of the people; and it must be plain to all of us that the home-life of our land is being terribly undermined and endangered today. What with the telegraph, the telephone, the daily press, the automobile, the airplane, the radio and the movies, what, with all these, shall be the outcome for the home? I repeat, the serious-minded person with eyes half open must be aware that the home-life of our land is being terribly imperiled and undermined. Urgent indeed is the summons that all of us be deeply concerned as to the homes of our nation. Whoever or whatever strikes at the home-life of the people strikes at the very heart of a worthy and stable civilization.

A Family Crisis

Here in our text Jacob had come to a crisis, a very definite crisis in the life of his own family. Such crisis hours come sooner or later to most families. Jacob waked up as one out of a terrible dream to the realization of the awful drift that had marked his own steps and the steps of his household.

Thirty years before, Jacob had fled from his brother Esau, whom he had cruelly wronged, whose birthright he had taken by fraud. He had to flee from his homeland into a far country. Goaded by conscience and tormented by fear, he fled far to the north. As night came on he laid down to sleep and took of the stones to make a pillow for his head. In his troubled sleep he had a vivid dream in which he saw a ladder reaching from earth to heaven, and on it angels ascending and descending. And God stood above the ladder and spoke wonderful words of comfort and promise to the weary and lonely fugitive.

When Jacob awoke he was filled with fear. He said, "Surely God is in this place; and I knew it not. This is none other than the house of God, and this the gate of heaven." So he arose and took the stone that he had put

under his head, and set it up as a kind of a[
poured oil on the top of it. He called the place
which means "house of God." There he made a gr___ .ow
to God. If God would go with him and be with him in the
way wherein he went and would take care of him, would
give him food and raiment and would bring him back in
safety to his father's land, then God should surely be his
God and he would surely devote one tenth of all his gains
unto God.

A Vow Forgotten

That dream and that vow unto God marked a high
peak in the experience of Jacob. But he, like others since
him, forgot his vow. The Bible faithfully tells us that he
let at least thirty years go by before he seriously set about
keeping that solemn vow made in early manhood. The
troubles and evils which beset him and his family in the
after years forced him to a realization of his shameful
neglect of the sacred vow he had made at Bethel.

The one girl in the family, Dinah, had been betrayed
and shamed. Her brothers, terribly moved by their sister's shame, sought to avenge her. On every hand feuds
and bitternesses were in evidence. Jacob's family had gone
far down the toboggan slide, and he woke up to a realization of it as a man stirs out of some horrible dream. He
realized, as the prodigal realized in the far country, the
plight he was in and the plight his family was in; and in
that hour a great resolve came to Jacob. In his heart he
heard the voice of God calling unto him to go back to
Bethel, the place of vision and dedication in his early life.
He resolved to go to Bethel and there renew his vows. He
would amend his own ways and seek spiritual blessings
for his family. Hear the appeal he made to them. He said
unto them, "Arise, let us go back to Bethel, change your
garments, be clean, put away the strange gods that are
among you; let us go back to Bethel and I will build an
altar there where God met me in the long ago, where I
made a great vow which I have failed to keep. I'll go back
now and build a real altar there and I want all of you to
go with me." This great scene, one of the most moving

scenes in all the Word of God, presents vital lessons which we will do well to consider this morning.

A Great Exhortation

First, let us note the exhortation Jacob gave his family. "Arise, let us go back to Bethel, be ye clean, change your garments; put away the strange gods that are among you and let us go back to Bethel where God met me long ago, and where I made Him a vow which I have neglected to keep. That vow I desire to renew at Bethel and begin even now keeping the promises I made to God in the long ago." A great exhortation! There are certain things about it that are very impressive. It was made in obedience to the command of God. God said to Jacob, "Arise, and go back to Bethel where I met thee long ago and where thou didst make a great vow to me." Jacob made this call to his family in response to the command of God.

Oh, what a great thing it is to obey the command of God. "Our wills are ours, we know not how, our wills are ours to make them Thine." Behold, to obey is better than sacrifice. Obedience to Christ—that is the governing principle in His kingdom. "Ye are my friends if ye do whatsoever I command." Our Lord and Master is Christ and His commands are to be implicitly obeyed. That was a pungent thing the immortal John Wesley said to a group of his younger fellow-workers, "The rules that I have made for you are to be *minded* by you and not *mended* by you." Now if Wesley felt it important to say that, certainly with all definiteness and positiveness Christ could say, "These commandments I announce, these principles I annunciate are to be minded by you." Whatsoever He sayeth unto you, do it!

So Jacob was obeying the command of God and he was taking his proper place as the head of the family, the high priest of the family.

Napoleon said in a critical time in the life of France, "What France needs now is good mothers." He should have added also, "and good fathers"; for good mothers and fathers are needed by every country. The father cannot abdicate his responsibility at all. If the father seeks to leave the rearing of the children to the mother, the father will be a great defaulter in the sight of the people and especially in the sight of God.

Jacob took his true place and said to his family, "Put away your strange gods; change your garments; be clean now and let us all go back to Bethel where I met God and where I made Him a great vow, which I have not kept." It was a great hour, a crisis hour in the life of this man Jacob. Go over it again. Thirty years before, that vow had been made; and it had not been kept. And trouble thick and fast had accumulated in the family of Jacob. An awful situation had developed in that family. Then it was that Jacob, the head of the family, stirred as one in a bad dream and said, "The hour has come for reparation; the hour has come for reformation; the hour has come for a decisive and radical change; let us go back to Bethel; let us seek to repair what ought to be repaired; to undo what ought to be undone; to carry out what God would have this family do." It was a great hour!

A Solemn Inventory Needed

It is my deepest conviction that that is the step supremely needed now by homes throughout America. Like Jacob, we should take stock of our moral and spiritual condition, a full and faithful inventory of our homes. We parents should hold solemn and loving interviews with every member of our families and households and seek as best we can to lead them into paths of truth and righteousness, paths which in many cases would take us and them back to the Bethel of past visions and vows where may be found new experiences of God's grace and mercy and power. And especially should Christian men who are fathers accept the God-given responsibilities which are theirs as heads and priests of the family. Oh, Christian fathers, have you been careless and forgetful and unfaithful as Jacob of old was for so many years? May God enable you even now to turn over a new leaf, to go back to your Bethel, to accept your responsibility as head of the family, to renew your vows and enter upon a new life of victory.

I give it, I say, as my deepest conviction that the supreme need for America today is to look again with all diligence and carefulness and conscientiousness to the home-life of the people. The father who can sleep easily with his boy trifling with the drink cup; oh, he needs to be aroused by the arousing power of God. The mother who can be calm and quiet with her daughter adopting habits that are leading toward an ill-ordered life, that mother needs to come back to her Bethel and look again at the deep meaning of parenthood and the responsibilities connected therewith. We need to go back to Bethel. Every home in this country should have a fresh inventory of its true status in the sight of God and if there are strange gods in our homes, if there are standards in our homes which would make us blush if Jesus should visit our homes, oh, if we have anything that would bring the blush of shame and humiliation to our cheeks by the visible presence of Jesus among us, let us clean it out, let us change our garments, let us put away our strange gods, let us go back in truth to Bethel and meet God. This is the great need of America today, in my humble judgment.

A nation is revealed by its home-life and no nation will rise any higher than the home-life of its people. If the home-life of the people be marked by bad standards, by doubtful practices, by low conduct, then the whole social order is involved to an awful degree, because we are bound together in the bundle of life. This man Jacob gave the right exhortation to his family. Every parent should say with Jacob, "Let us go back to that great crisis hour when we once vitally and mightily dealt with God and where in that holy place we vowed a great vow and registered a great resolve of soul, which we have forgotten to an awful degree. We should go back to our Bethel, the place of vision and of high resolve."

Notice again what Jacob said, "I am going back to Bethel and build a real altar of God there after these long thirty years." Let that resolve become personal with you and me. What about our altars unto God? What about the vows we made back yonder? What about the vow we made when the loved one was dreadfully ill and we went away into the secret place and poured out our prayer to God and made our vows? What about those vows? What about the promise you made when suddenly you faced a great crisis and all you could exclaim was, "Oh, God! Oh, dear God, help me! Oh, God, if you will help me, I promise I will do so and so"? Have you kept that promise?

What did you do with the vow about church attendance? Everybody ought to go to church. This applies especially to men and women who say they are Christians. What did you do with that vow about prayer meeting attendance and about Bible study in the Bible school? What have you done with the resolve you made: "I'm going to try my best to win souls for Christ, weak and frail though I am"? Have you forgotten that Christ gave soul-winning first place in His command to His followers?

The Place of Prayer

Are your personal altars still standing? Let us look at some of these altars. What about the altar of secret prayer? How much do you pray in secret? Did you pray today when the morning light broke in upon you with all its freshness and beauty? Then later, as you came to the house of God, did you pray in secret? For whom and what did you pray? What about the altar of secret prayer? What has become of it? Jesus said, "But thou, when thou prayest, enter into thy closet, and when thou hast shut thy door, pray to thy Father which is in secret; and thy Father which seeth in secret shall reward thee openly."

It was when Moses dared to be alone with God that God gave him the sight of that bush which burned and was not consumed. It was when Isaiah dared to be alone with God that God gave him a threefold vision that literally transformed the young prophet's life. It was when Jacob was alone with God yonder beside the brook Jabbok that he met God in a way never to be forgotten and had a blessing from God more gracious than human speech can describe. It is when you and I dare to be alone with God in the quiet place that we tell Him what we really hope for and desire and what we want to be and do before His face.

What have we done with the altar of family prayer? What if I ask now, "How many in this large throng within these walls and the larger throng listening in radio land, what have you done about the altar of family prayer? How many of you have family prayer? How many of you make it a point once a day to assemble the whole house together, children, servants if you have them, and all make humble, grateful acknowledgment unto God, the Giver of all good, for His mercy to you; and seek His guidance continuing and His favor unfailing for the unfolding days ahead? What have we done with family prayer? How can any Christian father be willing for his family to be reared, for his children to take their cue from him and to be to an awful degree molded by him, without having family prayer? What have you done about that? Some of us can testify that the blessings which came to us around the family altars in our childhood homes are more vivid and living and challenging than any of the other blessings we remember from those early years. What are we doing in these days about family prayers?

Many men are listening to me now who ought to say something like this today, "Frail and infirm and unworthy as I am, the altar of family prayer shall be established in my home; and once a day for a few minutes at least we will pause and let God speak to us out of His Word and then we will speak to Him out of our deepest heart through the blessed medium of prayer." Some of you men will likely say, "Preacher, we do not have time for family prayers." And I say to you that you had better find time for communion with God daily in your home. It will be the best investment of time for you and your household that you could possibly make, provided you approach it as a blessed privilege rather than as an irksome duty. It need not take much time, just a few minutes of the day for you and yours, especially for those growing children. Try it! I believe that you and your family will soon come to regard those minutes as the best of the day.

What have you done about the altar of church prayer? Oh, the decline if we allow the altar of church prayer to break down, to be indefinite and uncertain. The early

Corporate prayer

churches gave primacy to prayer and the whole Roman Empire was shaken to its foundations because they did just that. And any church that will give the primacy to prayer today will be visited with the merciful visitations and favor of God and the people round about will say of such a church, "We perceive of a truth that God is with these people."

Let us go back and set up the altar, that altar of secret prayer. Nobody can do your praying for you, my brother, nobody but you can do that. Let us set up the altar of family prayer. Let us summon the children around us and say, "My dear children, I ought to have done this before, but I have been timid about it. I do not feel that I am anywhere near a saint, but I want you to forgive me for my neglect, my dereliction and share with me now sympathetically and cooperatively as we set up a family altar to God from whom all blessings flow."

Let us magnify the altar of church prayer. Think of a deacon being absent from prayer meeting, unless hindered providentially. Think of a Sunday School teacher being absent for the appointed hour of prayer, when heartfelt pleas are made unto God in behalf of so many needy people and causes which are dear to the heart of God. Do not forget that prayer changes things. Prayer is the greatest power available to mortals. It can move the arm of God Almighty.   1 – 1000, 2 – 10,000 – and so on

A Family Returns

Take one more look at Jacob's return to Bethel. He frankly stated the case to his family and said, "Will you go back with me?" Under that brave proposal the whole turbulent and worldly group went back with their father. When a man acts honestly, humbly and faithfully, when a man is true to his Lord, marvelous results are sure to follow. The whole family went back with him. What else? When they went, the terror of the Lord was on all the cities through which they passed and the men of those cities did not follow after them to pursue them. When a man's ways please the Lord He maketh even his enemies to be at peace with him. "No weapon that is formed against thee shall prosper; and every tongue which rises against thee in judgment thou shalt condemn. This is the heritage of the servants of the Lord, and their righteousness is of Me, saith the Lord." At last, Jacob retraced his steps after long neglect and his family was recovered and great blessings came to Jacob and his family during the after years.

Surely the lesson is plain. Will we heed it? Will we heed it without delay? Oh, if it were the last word I had to say to my people and to my friends and to a needy world I would speak to you about your homes. Focus your best of head and heart on your homes today and through all the tomorrows! Why not begin even now by registering your high and holy decision for Christ and His church?

Who tells us today, "I would like to link my life with this church, coming by letter, or coming upon statement, having you send and get my letter"? Or who says, "I would like today to make my surrender to Christ who alone can save and who hath said, 'Him that cometh to me I will in no wise cast out'; I would like today to yield my life to this unforgetting and divine helper, Jesus, who died on the cross for sinners and therefore, died for me; for I am well aware, poignantly aware, that I am a sinner in the sight of God; I want this divine Redeemer to be mine; I want this atoning Savior to be mine and I yield my life to Him today; I begin a new life with Him; I make my surrender to Him; I receive Him to be my Savior"? Who has heretofore made that surrender and now wants to link his or her life with this church? Come! Come now; and may God bless you in the coming!

NOTES

The Great Day of Family Religion

George Whitefield (1714-1770) was born in Gloucester, England, and educated at Pembroke College, Oxford. There he came under the influence of John and Charles Wesley, although Whitefield was more Calvinistic in doctrine than they. Ordained in the Anglican Church, he quickly gained a reputation as an effective preacher; but the Anglican churches disapproved of him because of his association with the Methodists. He began to preach to great crowds out of doors and led John Wesley to follow his example. Whitefield made seven visits to America and is recognized as one of the leaders of evangelism and spiritual awakening in American history.

This sermon is taken from *Memoirs of George Whitefield*, edited by John Gilles and published in 1837 by Hunt and Noyes.

George Whitefield

5

THE GREAT DAY OF FAMILY RELIGION

As for me and my house, we will serve the Lord (Joshua 24:15).

THESE WORDS CONTAIN the holy resolution of pious Joshua who having, in a most moving affectionate discourse, recounted to the Israelites what great things God had done for them in the verse immediately preceding the text, comes to draw a proper inference from what he had been delivering and acquaints them, in the most pressing terms, that since God had been so exceeding gracious unto them, they could do no less than out of gratitude for such uncommon favors and mercies dedicate both themselves and families to His service. "Now, therefore, fear the Lord, and serve him in sincerity and truth, and put away the gods which your fathers served on the other side of the flood." And by the same engaging motive does the prophet Samuel afterwards enforce their obedience to the commandments of God. "Only fear the Lord and serve him in truth with all your heart; for consider how great things he hath done for you" (1 Sam. 12:24). But then, that they might not excuse themselves (as too many might be apt to do) by his giving them a bad example or think he was laying heavy burdens upon them whilst he himself touched them not with one of his fingers, he tells them in the text, that whatever regard they might pay to the doctrine he had been preaching, yet he (as all ministers ought to do) was resolved to live up to and practice it himself: "Choose you therefore whom you will serve, whether the gods which your fathers served, or the gods of the Amorites, in whose land ye dwell: but as for me and my house, we will serve the Lord."

A resolution, this worthy of Joshua and no less becoming, no less necessary, for every true son of Joshua that is entrusted with the care and government of a family in our day; and, if it was ever seasonable for ministers to preach up or people to put in practice family religion, it was never more so than in the present age; since it is greatly to be feared that out of those many households that call themselves Christians, there are but few that serve God in their respective families as they ought.

It is true indeed, visit our churches and you may perhaps see something of the form of godliness still subsisting among us; but even that is scarcely to be met within private houses. So that were the blessed angels to come as in the patriarchal age and observe our spiritual economy at home, would they not be tempted to say, as Abraham to Abimelech, "Surely the fear of God is not in this place" (Gen. 20:11)?

How such a general neglect of family religion first began to overspread the Christian world is difficult to determine. As for the primitive Christians, I am positive it was not so with them. No, they had not so learned Christ as falsely to imagine religion was to be confined solely to their assemblies for public worship; but, on the contrary, behaved with such piety and exemplary holiness in their private families that St. Paul often styles their house a church. Salute such a one, says he, and the church which is in his house. And I believe we must forever despair of seeing a primitive spirit of piety revived in the world, till we are so happy as to see a revival of primitive family religion and persons unanimously resolving with good old Joshua, in the words of the text, *As for me and my house, we will serve the Lord.*

From which words, I shall beg leave to insist on these three things:

First, that it is the duty of every governor of a family to take care that not only he himself, but also that those committed to his charge, serve the Lord.

Secondly, I shall endeavor to show after what manner a governor and his household ought to serve the Lord. And,

Thirdly, I shall offer some motives, in order to excite all governors with their respective households, to serve the Lord in the manner that shall be recommended.

A Sacred Duty

And *first*, I am to show that it is the duty of every governor of a family to take care that not only he himself but also that those committed to his charge should serve the Lord.

And this will appear if we consider that every governor of a family ought to look upon himself as obliged to act in three capacities: as a prophet, to instruct; as a priest, to pray for and with; as a king, to govern, direct, and provide for them. It is true indeed, the latter of these, their kingly office, they are not so frequently deficient in, (nay, in this they are generally too solicitous); but as for the two former, their priestly and prophetic offices, like Gallio, they care for no such things. But however indifferent some governors may be about it, they may be assured that God will require a due discharge of these offices at their hands. For is, as the apostle argues, "he that does not provide for his own house," in temporal things, "has denied the faith and is worse than an infidel"; to what greater degree of apostasy must he have arrived who takes no thought to provide for the spiritual welfare of his family!

But farther, persons are generally very liberal of their invectives against the clergy and think they justly blame the conduct of that minister who does not take heed to and watch over the flock of which the Holy Spirit has made him overseer; but may not every governor of a family be in a lower degree liable to the same censure, who takes no thought for those souls who are committed to his charge? For every house is as it were a little parish, every governor (as was before observed) a priest, every family a flock; and if any of them perish through the governor's neglect, their blood will God require at His hands.

Were a minister to disregard teaching his people publicly and from house to house, and to excuse himself by saying that he had enough to do to work out his own salvation with fear and trembling without concerning himself with that of others; would you not be apt to think such a minister to be like the unjust judge, "One that neither feared God nor regarded man"? And yet odious as such a character would be, it is no worse than that governor of a family deserves who thinks himself obliged only to save his own soul without paying any regard to the souls of his household. For (as was above hinted) every house is as it were a parish, and every master is concerned to secure, as much as in him lies, the spiritual prosperity of everyone under his roof, as any minister whatever is obliged to look to the spiritual welfare of every individual person under his charge.

What precedents men who neglect their duty in this particular can plead for such omission, I cannot tell. Doubtless not the example of holy Job who was so far from imagining that he had no concern, as governor of a family, with anyone's soul but his own that the Scripture acquaints us, "When the days of his children's feasting were gone about, that Job sent and sanctified them, and offered burnt offerings, according to the number of them all; for Job said, it may be that my sons have sinned and cursed God in their hearts. Thus did Job continually." Nor can they plead the practice of good old Joshua, whom, in the text, we find as much concerned for his household's welfare as his own. Nor lastly, that of Cornelius, who feared God, not only himself, but with all his house. And were Christians but of the same spirit of Job, Joshua, and the Gentile centurion, they would act as Job, Joshua, and Cornelius did.

But alas! if this be the case, and all governors of families ought not only to serve the Lord themselves, but likewise to see that their respective households do so too; what will then become of those who not only neglect serving God themselves but also make it their business to ridicule and scoff at any of their house that do? Who are not content with "not entering into the kingdom of heaven themselves; but those also that are willing to enter in, they hinder." Surely such men are factors for the devil indeed. Surely their damnation slumbereth not. For although God, in His good providence, may suffer such stumbling-blocks to be put in His children's way, and suffer their greatest enemies to be those of their own households for a trial of their sincerity and improvement of their faith; yet we cannot but pronounce a woe against those masters "by whom such offenses come." For if those that only take care of their own souls can scarcely be saved, where will such monstrous profane and wicked governors appear?

But hoping there are but few of this unhappy stamp, proceed we now to the *second* thing proposed: to show after what manner a governor and his household ought to serve the Lord.

How to Serve the Lord

1. And the first thing I shall mention is reading the Word of God. This is a duty incumbent on every person. "Search the scriptures, for in them ye think ye have eternal life," is a precept given by our blessed Lord indifferently to all; but much more so ought every governor of a family to think it in a peculiar manner spoken to himself because (as has been already proved) he ought to look upon himself as a prophet and therefore, agreeably to such a character, bound to instruct those under his charge in the knowledge of the Word of God.

This we find was the order God gave to His peculiar people Israel, for thus speaks his representative Moses, "These words (that is the Scripture words), which I command thee this day, shall be in thy heart, and thou shalt teach them diligently unto thy children (that is, as it is generally explained, servants as well as children), and thou shalt talk of them when thou sittest in thy house" (Deut. 6:6,7). From whence we may infer that the only reason why so many neglect to read the words of Scripture diligently to their children is because the words of Scripture are not in their hearts; for if they were, out of the abundance of the heart their mouths would speak.

Besides, servants as well as children are, generally, very ignorant and mere novices in the laws of God. And how shall they know unless someone teaches them? And what more proper to teach them by, than the lively oracles of God, "which are able to make them wise unto salvation"? And who more proper to instruct them by these lively oracles than parents and masters, who (as has been more than once observed) are as much concerned to feed them with spiritual, as with bodily bread, day by day.

But if these things be so, what a miserable condition are those unhappy governors in, who are so far from feeding those committed to their care with the sincere milk of the Word to the intent they may grow thereby, that they neither search the Scriptures themselves nor are careful to explain them to others? Such families must be in a happy way indeed to do their master's will, who take such prodigious pains to know it! Would not one imagine that they had turned converts to the church of Rome; that they thought ignorance to be the mother of devotion; and that those were to be condemned as heretics who read their Bibles? And yet how few families are there among us who do not act after this unseemly manner! "But shall I praise them in this? I praise them not: Brethren, this thing ought not so to be."

2. Pass we on now to the second means whereby every governor and his household ought to serve the Lord, family prayer.

This is a duty though as much neglected, yet as absolutely necessary as the former. Reading is a good preparative for prayer, as prayer is an excellent means to render reading effectual. And the reason why every governor of a family should join both these exercises together is plain, because a governor of a family cannot perform his priestly office (which we before observed he is in some degree invested with) without performing this duty of family prayer.

We find it therefore remarked, when mention is made of Cain and Abel offering sacrifices, that they brought them. But to whom did they bring them? Why, in all probability to their father Adam, who as priest of the family was to offer sacrifice in their names. And so likewise ought every spiritual son of the second Adam, who is entrusted with the care of a household, to offer up the spiritual sacrifices of supplications and thanksgivings, acceptable to God through Jesus Christ in the presence and name of all who wait upon or eat meat at His table.

Thus we read our blessed Lord behaved when He tabernacled among us. For it is said often that He prayed with His twelve disciples which was then His little family. And He Himself has promised a particular blessing to joint supplications. "Wheresoever two or three are gathered together in my name, there am I in the midst of them." And again, "If two or three are agreed touching anything they shall ask, it shall be given them." And to this, that we are commanded by the apostle to pray always with all manner of supplication, which doubtless includes family prayer. And holy Joshua, when he set up the good resolution in the text that he and his household would serve the Lord, certainly resolved to pray with his family, which is one of the best testimonies they could give of their serving Him.

Besides, there are no families but what have some common blessings, of which they have been all partakers, to give thanks for; some common crosses and afflictions, which they are to pray against; some common sins, which they are all to lament and bewail. But how this can be done without joining together in one common act of humiliation, supplication, and thanksgiving is difficult to devise.

From all which considerations put together, it is evident that family prayer is a great and necessary duty; and consequently, those governors who neglect it are certainly without excuse. And it is much to be feared, if they live without family prayer, they live without God in the world.

And yet, such a hateful character as this is, it is to be feared that were God to send out an angel to destroy us as He did once to destroy the Egyptian first born, and withal give Him a commission, as then, to spare no houses but where they saw the blood on the lintel sprinkled on the door post, so now, to let no families escape but those that called upon Him in morning and evening prayer; few would remain unhurt by His avenging sword. Shall I term such families Christians or heathens, doubtless they deserve not the name of Christians; and heathens will surely rise up in judgment against such profane families of this generation; for they had always their household gods whom they worshiped, and whose assistance they frequently invoked. And a pretty pass those families surely are arrived at, who must be sent to school to pagans. But will not the Lord be avenged on such profane households as these? Will He not pour out His fury upon those that call not upon His name?

3. But it is time for me to hasten to the third and last means I shall recommend whereby every governor ought with his household to serve the Lord, catechizing and instructing their children and servants, and bringing them up in the nurture and admonition of the Lord.

That this, as well as the two former, is a duty incumbent on every governor of a house appears from that famous encomium or commendation God gives of Abraham: "I know that he will command his children and his household after him, to keep the way of the Lord to do justice and judgment." And indeed scarce anything is more frequently pressed upon us in the holy writ, than this duty of catechizing. Thus, says God, in a passage before cited, "Thou shalt teach these words diligently to thy children." And parents are commanded in the New Testament, "to train up their children in the nurture and admonition of the Lord." The holy Psalmist acquaints us that one great end why God did such great wonders for His people was, "to the intent that when they grew up, they should show their children, or servants, the same." And in Deuteronomy 6 at the 20th and following verses, God strictly commands His people to instruct their children in the true nature of the ceremonial worship, when they should inquire about, as He supposed they would do, in time to come. And if servants and children were to be instructed in the nature of Jewish rites, much more ought they now to be initiated and grounded in the doctrines and first principles of the gospel of Christ; not only because it is a revelation which has brought life and immortality to a fuller and clearer light, but also because many seducers are gone abroad into the world who do their utmost endeavor to destroy not only the superstructure, but likewise to sap the very foundation of our most holy religion.

Would then the present generation have their posterity be true lovers and honorers of God, masters and parents must take Solomon's good advice and train up and catechize their respective households in the way wherein they should go?

I am aware but of one objection that can, with any show of reason, be urged against what has been advanced; which is, that such a procedure as this will take up too much time and hinder families too long from their worldly business. But it is much to be questioned whether persons that start such an objection are not of the same hypocritical spirit as the traitor Judas, who had indignation against devout Mary for being so profuse of her ointment in anointing our blessed Lord and asked why it might not be sold for two hundred pence and given to the poor. For has God given us so much time to work for ourselves, and shall we not allow some small pittance of it, morning and evening, to be devoted to His more immediate worship and service? Have not people read that it is God who gives men power to get wealth, and therefore that the best way to prosper in the world is to secure His favor? And has not our blessed Lord Himself promised that if we seek first the kingdom of God and His righteousness, all outward gifts shall be added unto us?

Abraham, no doubt, was a man of as great business as such objectors may be; but yet he would find time to command his household to serve the Lord. Nay, David was a king and consequently had a great deal of business upon his hands; yet notwithstanding, he professes that he would walk in his house with a perfect heart. And, to instance but one more, holy Joshua was a person certainly engaged very much in temporal affairs; and yet he solemnly declares before all Israel that as for him and his household, they would serve the Lord. And did persons but redeem their time as Abraham, David, or Joshua did, they would no longer complain that family duties kept them too long from the business of the world.

Motives for Service

But my *third* and last general head under which I was to offer some motives in order to excite all governors with their respective households to serve the Lord in the manner before recommended, I hope will serve, instead of a thousand arguments, to prove the weakness and folly of any such objection.

And the first motive I shall mention is *the duty of gratitude*, which you that are governors of families owe to God. Your lot, everyone must confess, is cast in a fair ground; providence has given you a goodly heritage above many of your fellow creatures; and therefore, out of a principle of gratitude, you ought to endeavor, as much as in you lies, to make every person of your respective households to call upon Him as long as they live; not to mention that the authority with which God has invested you as parents and governors of families is a talent committed to your trust and which you are bound to improve to your Master's honor. In other things we find governors and parents can exercise lordship over their children and servants readily, and frequently enough can say to one, Go, and he goes; and to another, Come, and he comes; to a third, Do this, and he does it. And shall this power be so often employed in your own affairs and never exerted in the things of God? Be astonished, O heavens, at this!

Thus did not faithful Abraham; no, God says that He knew Abraham would "command his servants and children after him." Thus did not Joshua; no, he was resolved not only to walk with God Himself, but to improve his authority in making all about him do so too; *As for me and my household, we will serve the Lord*. Let us go and do likewise.

But *secondly*, if gratitude to God will not, methinks *love* and pity to your children should move you, with your respective families, to serve the Lord.

Most people express a great fondness for their children, nay, so great, that very often their own lives are wrapped up in those of their offspring. "Can a woman forget her sucking child, that she should not have compassion on the son of her womb?" says God by his prophet Isaiah. He speaks of it as a monstrous thing and scarcely credible; but the words immediately following affirm it to be possible; yea, they may forget; and experience also assures us they may. Father and mother may both forsake their children, for what greater degree of forgetfulness can they express toward them, than to neglect the improvement of their better part and not bring them up in the knowledge and fear of God?

It is true indeed, parents seldom forget to provide for their children's bodies, (though, it is to be feared, some men are so far sunk beneath the beasts that perish as to neglect even that) but then how often do they forget, or rather, when do they remember to secure the salvation of their immortal souls? But is this their way of expressing their fondness for the fruit of their bodies? Is this the best testimony they can give of their affection to the darling of their hearts? Then was Delilah fond of Samson, when she delivered him up into the hands of the Philistines; then were those ruffians well affected to Daniel when they threw him into the den of lions.

But *thirdly*, if neither gratitude to God nor love and pity to your children will prevail on you; yet let a principle of *common honesty and justice* move you to set up the holy resolution in the text.

This is a principle which all men would be thought to act upon. But certainly, if any may be truly censured for their injustice, none can be more liable to such censure than those who think themselves injured if their servants withdraw themselves from their bodily work, and yet they in return take no care of their inestimable souls. For is it just that servants should spend their time and strength in their masters' service, and masters not at the same time give them what is just and equal for their service!

It is true, some men may think they have done enough when they give unto their servants food and raiment, and say, did not I bargain with thee for so much a year? But if they give them no other reward than this, what do they less for their very beasts? But are not servants better than they? Doubtless they are; and however masters may put off their convictions for the present, they will find a time will come when they shall know they ought to have given them some spiritual as well as temporal wages; and the cry of those who have mowed down their fields will enter into the ears of the Lord of Sabbath.

But *fourthly*, if neither gratitude of God, pity of children, nor a principle of common justice to servants are sufficient to balance all objections; yet let that darling, that prevailing motive of *self-interest* turn the scale and engage you with your respective households to serve the Lord.

This weighs greatly with you in other matters; be then persuaded to let it have a due and full influence on you in this; and if it has, if you have but faith as a grain of mustard seed, how can you avoid believing that promoting family religion would be the best means to promote your own temporal as well as eternal welfare? For "godliness has the promise of the life that now is, as well as that which is to come."

Besides, you all, doubtless, wish for honest servants and pious children; and to have them prove otherwise, would be as great a grief to you as it was to Elisha to have a treacherous Gehazi, or David to be troubled with a rebellious Absalom. But how can it be expected they should learn their duty, except those set over them take care to teach it to them? Is it not as reasonable to expect you should reap where you had not sown, or gather where you had not strewed?

Did Christianity, indeed, give any countenance to children and servants to disregard their parents and masters according to the flesh or represent their duty to them as inconsistent with their entire obedience to their Father and Master who is in heaven, there might then be some pretense for neglecting to instruct them in the principles of such a religion. But since the precepts of this pure and undefiled religion are all of them holy, just, and good; and the more they are taught their duty to God, the better they will perform their duties to you; methinks to neglect the improvement of their souls out of a dread of spending too much time in religious duties is acting quite contrary to your own interests as well as duty.

Fifthly and lastly, if neither gratitude to God, love to your children, common justice to your servants, nor even that most prevailing motive, self-interest, will excite; yet let *a consideration of the terrors of the Lord* persuade you to put in practice the pious resolution in the text. Remember, the time will come, and that perhaps very shortly, when we must all appear before the judgment seat of Christ where we must give a solemn and strict account how we have had our conversation, in our respective families, in this world. How will you endure to see your children and servants (who ought to be your joy and crown of rejoicing in the day of the Lord Jesus Christ) coming out as so many swift witnesses against you; cursing the father that begot them, the womb that bare them, the paps which they have sucked, and the day they ever entered into your houses? Think you not the damnation which men must endure for their own sins will be sufficient, that they need load themselves with the additional guilt of being accessory to the damnation of others also? O consider this, all ye that forget to serve the Lord with your respective households, "lest he pluck you away, and there be none to deliver you!"

But God forbid, brethren, that any such evil should befall you. No, rather will I hope that you have been in some measure convinced by what has been said of the great importance of family religion and therefore are ready to cry out, in the words immediately following the text, "God forbid that we should forsake the Lord"; and again, verse 21: "nay, but we will (with our several households) serve the Lord."

And that there may be always such a heart in you, let me exhort all governors of families, in the name of our Lord Jesus Christ, often to reflect on the inestimable worth of their own souls, and the infinite ransom, even, the precious blood of Jesus Christ, which has been paid down for them. Remember that you are fallen creatures; that you are by nature lost and estranged from God: and that you can never be restored to your primitive happiness, till by being born again of the Holy Spirit, you arrive at your primitive state of purity, have the image of God re-stamped upon your souls, and thereby made meet to be partakers of the inheritance with the saints in light. Do, I say, but seriously and frequently reflect on and act as persons that believe such important truths, and you will no more neglect your family's spiritual welfare than your own. No, the love of God, which will then be shed abroad in your hearts, will constrain you to do your utmost to preserve them. And the deep sense of God's free grace in Christ Jesus, (which you will then have) in calling you, will excite you to do your utmost to save others, especially those of your own household. And though, after all your pious endeavors, some may continue unreformed; yet you will have this comfortable reflection to make, that you did what you could to make your families religious and therefore may rest assured of setting down in the kingdom of heaven with Abraham, Joshua, and Cornelius, and all the godly householders who in their several generations shone forth as so many lights in their respective households upon earth. *Amen.*

NOTES

Address to Parents

Dwight Lyman Moody (1837-1899) is known around the world as one of America's most effective evangelists. Converted as a teenager through the witness of his Sunday School teacher, Moody became active in YMCA and Sunday School work in Chicago while pursuing a successful business career. He then devoted his full time to evangelism and was mightily used of God in campaigns in both the United States and Great Britain. He founded the Northfield School for girls, the Mount Hermon School for boys, the Northfield Bible Conference, and the Moody Bible Institute in Chicago. Before the days of planes and radio, Moody traveled more than a million miles and addressed more than 100 million people.

This message is from *The Gospel Awakening* (Chicago: J. Fairbanks & Co., 1879).

Dwight Lyman Moody

6

ADDRESS TO PARENTS

> Oh that there were such an heart in them, that they would fear me, and keep all my commandments always, that it might be well with them, and with their children forever (Deuteronomy 5:29).

I want to call your attention to Deuteronomy 5:29. "Oh that there were such a heart in them, that they would fear me, and keep all my commandments always, that it might be well with them, and with their children forever." And also the 6th chapter and 7th verse: "And thou shalt teach them diligently unto thy children, and shalt talk of them when thou sittest in thine house, and when thou walkest by the way, and when thou liest down, and when thou risest up." I used to think, when I was superintendent on the North Side, when I was laboring among the children and trying to get the parents interested to save their children, that if I ever did become a preacher I would have but one text and one sermon, and that should be addressed to parents; because when we get them interested, their interest will be apparent in the children. We used to say, if we get the lambs in, the old sheep will follow; but I didn't find that to be the case. When we got the children interested on one Sunday, the parents would be sometimes pulling the other way all the week, and before Sunday came again the impression that had been made would be gone; and I came to the conclusion that, unless we can get the parents interested, or could get some kind Christian to look after those children, it would almost be a sin to bring them to Christ. If there is no one to nurse them, to care for them and just to water the seed, why they are liable to be drawn away, and when they grow up, to be far more difficult to reach.

I wish to say tonight that I am as strong as ever upon sudden conversion, and there are a great many ministers, a great many parents, who scoff and laugh when they hear of children who have been brought unto Christ at these meetings. Now, in many of the churches the sermons go over their heads; they don't do the young any good; they don't understand the preaching; and if they are impressed here, we ought not to discourage them. My friends, the best thing we can do is to bring them early to Christ. These earliest impressions never, never leave them; and I do not know why they should not grow up in the service of Christ. I contend that those who are converted early are the best Christians. Take the man who is converted at fifty. He has continually to fight against his old habits; but take a young man or a young girl, and they get a character to form and a whole long life to give to Christ. An old man unconverted got up in an inquiry meeting recently, and said he thought we were very hard-hearted down in the Tabernacle; we went right by when we saw some young person. He thought, as he was old, he might be snatched away before these young people; but with us it seemed as if Christ was of more importance to the young than the old. I confess truly that I have that feeling. If a young man is converted, he perhaps has a long life of fifty years to devote to Christ; but an old man is not worth much. Of course, his soul is worth much; but he is not worth much for labor.

Hold Up the Cross

While down at a convention in Illinois, an old man got up, past seventy years; he said he remembered but one thing about his father, and that one thing followed him all through life. He could not remember his death, he had no recollection of his funeral; but he recollected his father one winter night, taking a little chip, and with his pocket-knife whittling out a cross, and with the tears in his eyes he held up that cross and told how God in his infinite love sent his Son down here to redeem us, how He had died on the cross for us. The story of the cross followed him through life; and I tell you, if you teach children these truths, they will follow them through life. We have so much unbelief among us, like those disciples when they rebuked the people for bringing the children to Christ; but He said: "Suffer little children to come unto Me, and forbid them not, for of such is the kingdom of heaven."

I heard of a Sunday School concert at which a little child of eight was going to recite. Her mother had taught her, and when the night came the little thing was trembling so she could hardly speak. She commenced, "Jesus said," and completely broke down. Again she tried it, "Jesus said, suffer," but she stopped once more. A third attempt was made by her, "suffer little children—and don't anybody stop them, for He wants them all to come"; and that is the truth. There is not a child who has parents in the Tabernacle but He wants, and if you bring them in the arms of your faith, and ask the Son of God to bless them and train them in the knowledge of God, and teach them as you walk your way, as you lie down at night, as you rise up in the morning, they will be blessed.

But I can imagine some skeptic in yonder gallery saying, "That's well enough, but it is all talk. Why I have known children of ministers and Christian people who have turned out worse than others." I've heard that all my life; but I tell you that is one of the devil's lies. I will admit I've heard of many Christian people having bad children, but they are not the worst children. That was tested once. A whole territory was taken in which fathers and mothers were Christians, and it was found that two-thirds of the children were members of churches; but they took a portion of country where all the fathers and mothers were not Christians, and it was found that not one in twelve of the children attended churches. That was the proportion.

God Has No Grandchildren

Look at a good man who has had a bad son. Do you want to know the reason? In the first place, children do not inherit grace. Because fathers and mothers are good, that is no reason why their children should be good. Children are not born good. Men may talk of natural goodness, but I don't find it. Goodness must come down from the Father of Light. To have a good nature, a man must be born of God. There is another reason—a father may be a very good man, but the mother may be pulling in another way. She may be ambitious, and may want her children to occupy a high worldly position. She has some high ambition and trains the child for the world. Again, it may be the reverse—a holy, pious mother and a worldly father; and it is pretty hard when father and mother do not pull together.

Another reason is, and you will excuse me the expression, but a great many people have very little sense about bringing up children. Now, I've known mothers who punish their children by making them read the Bible. Do not be guilty of such a thing. If you want children not to hate the Bible, do not punish them by making them read it. It is the most attractive book in the world. But that is the way to spoil its attractiveness and make them hate it with a perfect hate. There is another reason. A great many people are engaged in looking after other people's children and neglecting their own. No father or mother has a right to do this, whatever may be the position they hold in the world. The father may be a statesman, or a great businessman; but he is responsible for his children. If they do not look after their children, they will have to answer for it some day. There will be a blight in their paths, and their last days will be very bitter.

Teach Them Diligently

There are a great many reasons which I might bring forward, if I had time, why good people's children turn out bad; but let me say one word about bringing up these children, how to train them in Christian ways. The Word is very plain, "Teach them diligently." In the street cars, as we go about our business night and morning, talk of Christ and heavenly things. It seems to me as if these things were the last things many of us think about, and as if Christ was banished from our homes. A great many people have a good name as Christians. They talk about ministers and Sunday Schools, and will come down and give a dinner to the bootblacks, and seem to be strong patrons of the cause of Christ; but when it comes to talking to children personally about Christ, that is another thing. The Word is very plain, "Teach them diligently"; and if we want them to grow up a blessing to the Church of God and to the world, we must teach them.

I can imagine some of you saying: "It may be very well for Mr. Moody to lay down theories, but there are a great many difficulties in the way." I heard of a minister who said he had the grandest theory upon the bringing up of children. God gave him seven children, and he found that his theory was all wrong. They were all differently constituted. I will admit that this is one difficulty; but if our heart is set upon this one thing—to have our children in glory—God will give us all the light we need. He is not going to leave us in darkness. If that is not the aim of your heart, make it this very night. I would rather, if I went tonight, leave my children in the hope of Christ than leave them millions of money. It seems to me as if we were too ambitious to have them make a name, instead of to train them up for the life they are to lead forever.

And another thing about government. Never teach them revenge. If a baby falls down on the floor, don't give it a book with which to strike the floor. They have enough of revenge in them without being taught it. Then don't teach them to lie. You don't like that; but how many parents have told their children to go to the door, when they did not want to see the visitor, and say, "Mother is not in." That is a lie.

Children are very keen to detect. They very soon see those lies, and this lays the foundation for a good deal of trouble afterward. "Ah," some of you say, "I never do this." Well, suppose some person comes in that you don't want to see. You give him a welcome, and when he goes you entreat him to stay; but the moment he is out of the door you say, "What a bore!"

The children wonder at first; but they very soon begin to imitate father and mother. Children are very good imitators. A father and mother never ought to do a thing that they don't want their children to do. If you don't want them to smoke, don't you smoke; if you don't want them to chew, don't you chew; if you don't want them to play billiards, don't you play billiards; if you don't want them to drink, don't you drink, because children are grand imitators.

A lady once told me that she was in her pantry on one occasion, and she was surprised by the ringing of the bell. As she whirled round to see who it was, she broke a tumbler. Her little child was standing there, and she thought her mother was doing a very correct thing, and the moment the lady left the pantry, the child commenced to break all the tumblers she could get hold of. You may laugh, but children are very good imitators.

If you don't want them to break the Sabbath day, keep it holy yourself; if you want them to go to church, go to church yourself. It is very often by imitation that they utter their first oath, that they tell their first lie, and then this act grows upon them; and when they try to quit the habit, it has grown so strong upon them that they cannot do it.

How Old Should They Be?

"Ah," some say, "we do not believe in children being converted. Let them grow up to manhood and woman-hood, and then talk of converting them." They forget that in the meantime their characters are formed, and per-haps they have commenced to enter the dens of infamy; and when they have arrived at manhood and woman-hood, we find it is too late to alter their character. How unfaithful we are.

"Teach them diligently." How many parents in this vast assembly know where their sons are. Their sons may be in the halls of vice. Where does your son spend his eve-nings? You don't care enough for him to ascertain what kind of company he keeps, what kind of books he reads; you don't care whether he is reading those miserable, trashy novels or not, and getting false ideas of life. You don't know till it is too late. Oh, may God wake us up and teach us the responsibility devolving upon us in training our children.

While in London, an officer in the Indian army, hearing of us being over there, said: "Lord, now is the time for my son to be saved." He got a furlough and left India, and came to London. When he came there for that purpose, of course, God was not going to let him go away without the blessing. How many men are interested in their sons enough to do as this man did? How many men are sufficiently interested in them to bring them here? How many parents stand in the way of the salvation of their children?

I don't know anything that discouraged me more, when I was superintendent on the North Side, than when, after begging with parents to allow their children to come to Sunday School—and how few of them came—whenever spring arrived those parents would take those children from the school, and lead them into those German gardens. And now a great many are reaping the consequences.

I remember one mother who heard that her boy was impressed at our meeting. She said her son was a good enough boy, and he didn't need to be converted. I pleaded with that mother, but all my pleading was of no account. I tried my influence with the boy; but while I was pulling one way she was pulling the other. Her influence prevailed. Naturally, it would. Well, to make a long story short, some time after I happened to be in the County Jail, and I saw him there. "How did you come here?" I asked; "does your mother know where you are?" "No, don't tell her; I came here under an assumed name, and I am going to Joliet for four years. Do not let my mother know of this," he pleaded; "she thinks I am in the army." I used to call on that mother, but I had promised her boy I would not tell her, and for four years she mourned over that boy. She thought he had died on the battlefield, or in a Southern hospital. What a blessing he might have been to that mother, if she had only helped us to bring him to Christ.

But that mother is only a specimen of hundreds and thousands of parents in Chicago. If we would have more family altars in our homes and train them to follow Christ, why the Son of God would lead them into "green pastures"; and instead of having sons who curse the mothers who gave them birth, they would bless their fathers and mothers. In the Indiana Penitentiary, I was told of a man who had come there under an assumed name. His mother heard where he was. She was too poor to ride there, and she footed it. Upon her arrival at the prison, she at first did not recognize her son in his prison suit and short hair; but when she did see who it was, that mother threw her arms around that boy and said: "I am to blame for this; if I had only taught you to obey God and keep the Sabbath, you would not have been here."

How many mothers, if they were honest, could attribute the ruination of their children to their early training. God has said, if we don't teach them those blessed commandments He will destroy us; and the law of God never changes. It does not only apply to those callous men who make no profession of religion, but to those who stand high in the church, if they make the same mistake.

The Example of Eli

Look at that high priest Eli. He was a good man and a kind one, but one thing he neglected to do—to train his children for God. The Lord gave him warning, and at last destruction came upon his house. Look at that old man ninety-eight years old, with his white hair, like some of the men on the platform, sitting in the town of Shiloh, waiting to hear the result of the battle. The people of Israel came into the town and took out the ark of God, and when it came into the camp a great shout went up to heaven, for they had the ark of their God among them. They thought they were going to succeed; but they had disobeyed God. When the battle came on they fought manfully, but no less than 30,000 of the Israelites fell by the swords of their enemies; and a messenger came running from the field through the streets of Shiloh to where Eli was, crying: "Israel is defeated, the ark is taken, and Hophni and Phineas have been slain in battle." And the old priest, when he heard it, fell backward by the side of the gate, and his neck broke and he died. Oh, what a sad ending to that man; and when his daughter-in-law heard the news, there was another death in that family recorded. In that house destruction was complete.

My friends, God is true; and if we do not obey Him in this respect, He will punish us. It is only a question of time. Look at King David. See him waiting for the tidings of the battle. He had been driven from his throne by his own son, whom he loved; but when the news came that he was slain, see how he cried: "O my son Absalom! would to God I had died for thee!" It was worse than death to him; but God had to punish him, because he did not train his son to love the Lord. My friends, if He punished Eli and David, He will punish you and me. May God forgive us for the past, and may we commence a new record tonight. My friends, if you have not a family altar, erect one tonight. Let us labor that our children may be brought to glory. Don't say children are too young. Mothers and fathers, if you hear your children have been impressed with religion, don't stand in the way of their conversion, but encourage them all you can.

A Mother's Story

While I was attending a meeting in a certain city some time ago, a lady came to me and said: "I want you to go home with me; I have something to say to you." When we reached her home, there were some friends there. After they had retired, she put her arms on the table, and tears began to come into her eyes, but with an effort she repressed her emotion. After a struggle, she went on to say that she was going to tell me something which she had never told any other living person. I should not tell it now, but she has gone to another world. She said she had a son in Chicago, and she was very anxious about him. When he was young, he became interested in religion at the rooms of the Young Men's Christian Association. He used to go out in the street and circulate tracts. He was her only son, and she was very ambitious he should make a name in the world and wanted to get him into the very highest circles. Oh, what a mistake people make about these highest circles. Society is false; it is a sham. She was deceived, like a good many more votaries of fashion and hunters after wealth at the present time. She thought it was beneath her son to go down and associate with those young men who hadn't much money. She tried to get him away from them, but they had more influence than she had; and, finally, to break off this old association, she packed him off to a boarding-school.

He went soon to Yale College, and she supposed he got into one of those miserable secret societies there that have ruined so many young men; and the next thing she heard was that the boy had gone astray. She began to write letters urging him to come into the kingdom of God; but she heard that he tore the letters up without reading them. She went to him, to try and regain whatever influence she possessed over him; but her efforts were useless, and she came home with a broken heart. He left New Haven, and for two years they heard nothing of him. At last they heard he was in Chicago; and his father found him, and gave him thirty thousand dollars to start in business. They thought it would change him; but it didn't.

They asked me when I went back to Chicago to try and use my influence with him. I got a friend to invite him to his house one night, where I intended to meet him; but he heard I was to be there and did not come near. Like a good many other young men, who seem to be afraid of me, I tried many times to reach him, but could not. While I was traveling one day on the New Haven railroad, I bought a New York paper, and in it I saw a dispatch saying he had been drowned in Lake Michigan. His father came on to find his body, and after considerable searching, he discovered it. All the clothes and his body were covered with sand. The body was taken home to that brokenhearted mother. She said, "If I thought he was in heaven, I would have peace." Her disobedience of God's law came back upon her.

So, my friends, if you have a boy impressed with the gospel, help him to come to Christ. Bring him in the arms of your faith, and He will unite you closer to him. Let us have faith in Him, and let us pray day and night that our children may be born of the Spirit.

NOTES

Love, Courtship & Marriage: Isaac and Rebekah—Jacob and Rachel

Clarence Edward Noble Macartney (1879-1957) ministered in Paterson, NJ, and Philadelphia, PA, before assuming the influential pastorate of First Presbyterian Church, Pittsburgh, PA, where he ministered for twenty-seven years. His preaching especially attracted men, not only to the Sunday services but also to his popular Tuesday noon luncheons. He was gifted in dealing with Bible biographies, and, in this respect, has well been called "the American Alexander Whyte." Much of his preaching was topical-textual, but it was always biblical, doctrinal and practical. Perhaps his most famous sermon is "Come Before Winter."

The sermon I have selected is taken from *The Way of a Man with a Maid*, reprinted in 1974 by Baker Book House.

Clarence Edward Noble Macartney

7

LOVE, COURTSHIP & MARRIAGE: ISAAC AND REBEKAH— JACOB AND RACHEL

Wilt thou go with this man? (Genesis 24:58).

And Jacob served seven years for Rachel; and they seemed unto him but a few days, for the love he had to her (Genesis 29:20).

SEPULCHERS AND MARRIAGE altars, burials and betrothals, how close together they come in life! The minister has hardly finished the words of committal, "Dust to dust, earth to earth, ashes to ashes," until he finds himself repeating to the man and the woman the vows of matrimony. So it has been from the beginning. Abraham buried Sarah his wife in the cave of Machpelah, and then turned to the business of securing a wife for Isaac. A few pages are turned, and it is Isaac who is being buried and his son, Jacob, who is being married. So it has gone on from the beginning, and so it will go on until the world is lifted to that state where they neither marry nor are given in marriage.

We have here the two most celebrated stories of love, courtship, and marriage in the Old Testament. In the one instance, that of Rebekah and Isaac, marriage came first, and then courtship and love. In the second instance, that of Jacob and Rachel, love and courtship came first, and marriage afterwards. But in both instances it was real love, real courtship, and true marriage.

Until time ends, the divine order is what God instituted from the beginning—that a man shall forsake his father and mother and cleave unto his wife, and they shall become one flesh. Here in this fundamental fact is the foundation of law, order, human society, the church, and the heavenly commonwealth. Without marriage, all of

81

these are impossible; and they who follow this original institute are helping to carry out the plan and the will of God in the world.

I. Isaac and Rebekah

This relationship is honored and perpetuated in the marriage service of the Church of England, where the bride and the groom are exhorted to live together "as Isaac and Rebekah lived faithfully together." Sarah had been a model wife and mother in that family circle. Isaac was past forty and not yet married. The reason seems to have been, first of all, a natural and rather attractive diffidence and passiveness of disposition; and in the second place, an unusual bond of close affection between this son of the promise and his mother and father. Then there was the fact that they were dwelling in the land of Canaan, which, although the promised land, was a land of idolaters, whose inhabitants, unless Abraham was willing to lower his standards, could supply no suitable candidates for the hand of Isaac.

Mixed Marriages

When Abraham is old and well stricken in years, he takes thought for the continuity and succession of his line through Isaac and plans for his marriage. Some would never take this step unless it were planned for them, and if all could plan as well as Abraham did, there could be little objection to such a manner of procedure. Abraham called his servant, the faithful Eleazer, who had been over his household for more than half a century, and charged him with an oath to go to Mesopotamia where Abraham's people lived and secure a suitable wife for Isaac. He made him swear to two things; first, that he would not let Isaac take a wife of the people of the land of Canaan, who were idolaters; and second, that he would not let Isaac go back to Mesopotamia, for thence Abraham, faithful to the command of God, had migrated. Therefore, it would not do for his son, to whom the promise was continued, to return to Mesopotamia.

The care which Abraham gave to the marriage of Isaac is to be commended to fathers and mothers today. He charges the one who is to arrange for this marriage that the woman chosen is to be of the same religion, the same race, and the same general family and social standing. Love imagines that it can overleap the barriers of race and blood and religion, and in the enthusiasm and ecstasy of choice these obstacles and barriers appear insignificant. But the facts of experience are against such an idea. Mixed marriages are rarely happy. Observation and experience demonstrate that the marriage of a Gentile and a Jew, a Protestant and a Catholic, an American and a foreigner, has less chance of a happy result than a marriage where the man and the woman are of the same race and religion. Abraham insists that Isaac shall marry a believing woman, and this condition is one which every Christian contemplating marriage should consider. There are not a few who feel that the rite of Christian marriage should be celebrated only when *both* the man and the woman are acknowledged and professed disciples of Christ, and where they undertake to make their home a Christian home and to associate themselves with a Christian church. There is something to be said for that position, for when one is not a professed Christian, the solemn vows made in Christ have little meaning and no binding power.

By an Ancient Well

Now the scene shifts to far-off Mesopotamia. With ten camels laden with presents and supplies, the servant of Eleazer has reached the city of Nahor. Probably that city was just a collection of adobe huts or scattered tents. But there was one refreshing place in it, and that was the ancient well outside the city. These wells then, and even today, were the meeting place for the people, and there the women gathered, not only to draw water, but to drink the water of social exchange and companionship. Just at the time that the women are coming out to draw water, Eleazer reaches his destination and makes his camels kneel down by the well. When he sees the women approaching with their waterpots upon their shoulders, he asks God to direct him by a sign to the right choice of a wife for Isaac. It is to be noted that this was no insignificant sign such as people sometimes ask for—a chance meeting, or a number in a series, or a certain color or form of an object—but one which carried with it an index to character. He would ask the first maiden who appeared to let down her pitcher and give him a drink of water, and if she responded to his request, and not only gave him water, but volunteered to draw water for his camels, then he would feel satisfied that this was the woman. The sign which he asked for was one which would indicate that the woman who thus responded had a heart of kindness, hospitality, and courtesy—always a pleasing thing in a woman.

The prayer of the servant had hardly been finished when Rebekah came out with her pitcher upon her shoulder, "and the damsel was very fair to look upon, a virgin; and she went down to the well and filled her pitcher and came up." As she came up the steps at the mouth of the well, the servant hurried to meet her and said, "Let me, I pray thee, drink a little water of thy pitcher." And Rebekah, with grace and courtesy, responded, "Drink, my lord," at the same time letting down her pitcher and drawing water for him. Then, when she had drawn for him, she volunteered to draw water for his camels. "The man, wondering," the narrative tells us, "held his peace," anxious to know whether the Lord had prospered his journey, and if this was to be the woman for Isaac. In silence he watches Rebekah as, with infinite grace in her lithe body and beautiful face, she bows herself to the task of drawing up the water for the thirsty camels, little thinking that at the same time she was weaving the threads of fate and destiny. So ever it is. When we are most self-conscious, our actions may be the least significant; and when we are acting as Rebekah did, spontaneously, naturally, without thought of the results or consequences, we are forging the links in the chain of our destiny.

"Whose daughter art thou?" the man said to Rebekah; and when he heard that she was the daughter of Bethuel and Nahor, and thus a niece of Abraham and a cousin to Isaac, he was overjoyed, and bowing himself down, wor-

shiped God, saying: "Blessed be the Lord God of my master Abraham, who hath not left destitute my master of
his mercy and truth: I being in the way, the Lord led me
to the house of my master's brethren."

We do not ask for signs just as this servant did. Yet in
the important steps of life and in marriage above all else,
because nothing affects one's life so much for better or
worse, it is right that we should wait upon God and ask
that He would make plain our path. This the servant of
Abraham had done all through his long journey. "I *being
in the way*," he said, "the Lord led me." People who do not
put themselves in the way, or who, in the way, get out of
it and follow their own way, need not be surprised if their
way leads them astray. With the upright, God has said,
He will show Himself upright; and with the froward He
will show Himself froward. If we stay in the way of His
commandments, we have a right to expect His blessing
and His leadership.

The Great Decision

Rebekah, with natural grace and hospitality, invites the
servant of Abraham to come and lodge in her father's house.
In the meantime, her brother, Laban, appears on the scene,
not yet the hard-boiled Laban of Jacob's romance, but a man
of true hospitality and brotherly interest and affection. The
camels are unharnessed and given straw and provender for
the night, while Eleazor and his companions go to the house
of Rebekah. The table is spread with such things as were in
the order of hospitality in those days; but this faithful servant knows the psychological moment and says that he will
not eat until he has stated his business. Then he rehearses
the family history; the birth of Isaac, the death of Sarah, the
charge which Abraham gave him, the journey of five hundred miles over the sands, his prayer by the well, and the
coming of Rebekah. He then asks point-blank whether or
not there is hope for his proposition. If there is not, he will
move on to some other collateral branch of Abraham's family. Laban and Bethuel both answered that the thing seems
to be of the Lord, and that if Rebekah is willing to go to be
the wife of Isaac, she can go. Then jewels and presents and

decorations are brought out of the servant's treasury to deck the beautiful Rebekah and the members of her family.

When morning dawns over the desert—and what were the dreams of Rebekah that night?—the servant is anxious to depart. Laban and Bethuel suggest a wait of ten days; perhaps that Rebekah might make more elaborate preparation as to her bridal garments; or perhaps that she might search and know her own mind better. But the wise servant says that now is the accepted time and insists upon an immediate departure. Then the father and brother turn to Rebekah and say those words which have echoed in the world ever since, and in the marriage service, "Wilt thou go with this man?" For her it meant an everlasting farewell to the town where she was born, to her girlhood friends, to the quiet evenings of chatter and gossip by the well; separation from father and mother, brother and sister, if she had any. There was silence for a moment, and then Rebekah made her answer, "I will go." She felt safe in going because the whole subject and matter had been advanced and proposed in the name of God.

If the unseen bridegroom was of the same mind as this servant, she knew then she was safe. And yet, after all, as in every such response, it had to be the answer of faith. Rebekah said, "I will go." How that answer has echoed upon the lips of thousands and thousands of the sisters of Rebekah! "Wilt thou go?" And back has come the answer, "I will go"— no doubt, to those who hear both sentences, earth's sweetest music. "I will go!" and she has gone, although it meant the crossing of broad seas, a hut in a land of savages, a rude frontier settlement, one room in the third story back, which must serve as bedroom, living room, and kitchen. "I will go!" although it has meant separation, loneliness, child-bearing, sickness, grief, sometimes disappointment, sorrow, and tragedy. Yet the world keeps on going because men ask, "Wilt thou go?" and women still answer with radiant eye and tremulous voice, "I will go."

Meditation and the Soul

The camels are off again, this time on the great trail to the southwest and the land of Canaan. During those days and nights of travel, Rebekah had plenty of time to think about her journey and her prospective bridegroom. At length they came to the well of Lahai-roi. It was toward the evening-tide, and Isaac had gone out into the fields to meditate. It is then, in that mystic period between the passing of the day and the oncoming of the night, that the mystery and stillness of the world invite thought and meditation. Meditation is the twilight of the soul, and it is at the eventide, when all nature whispers of the supernatural, and the temporal seems to reflect the eternal, that doors and windows are opened for us into the heavenly places. That was a promising thing about Isaac. He was not all on the surface. He had moments of introspection and meditation. Before a woman marries a man, it would be well to know whether or not he ever meditates; and the same holds true of a man before he marries a woman. On both sides, one ought to know whether with the other it is just a round of activities and pleasures and excitements and moving pictures and comic papers and cheap stories, or whether the soul of the man or the soul of the woman has twilight hours of meditation and of thought. Frivolity in one or both partners to a marriage is, as often as anything else, a source of weariness and distaste on one side or the other; for, as one has said, "A fly is as difficult to tame as a hyena."

The moment Rebekah discerned the form of the contemplating Isaac, with becoming humility and modesty, true to the customs of the East, she alighted from her camel and covered her beauties of face and form with the long veil which then, and even now, prevailed in the East. This veil was a token of modesty, and yet of confidence and intimacy, and has its survival in the veil which the bride wears at the weddings of our own day.

And He Loved Her

It must have been an anxious and critical moment for both Rebekah and Isaac. Suppose that the as yet unknown bridegroom should prove repellent to Rebekah? Or what if the bride should be distasteful to Isaac? But this was one of those marriages made in heaven, and the confidence of both Rebekah and Isaac was rewarded by mutual admiration and affection. Isaac dismissed the servant after he had related his story. Her nurse and companion, who thus far had been her chaperon, retired from the black tent; the veil was lifted from her face, and the romance which commenced in Mesopotamia ended in true happiness and true affection. Isaac took her into his mother Sarah's tent, the place sacred to him because of that great mother's memories; "and she became his wife, and he loved her; and Isaac was comforted after his mother's death." So, in keeping with the divine plan, how it is not good for the man to be alone, the solitary and mourning Isaac is comforted and companioned by this successor to his mother, who becomes his wife.

II. Jacob and Rachel

In the story of Jacob and Rachel, we have the way of a man with a maid which is more in keeping with the ideas of our day and generation. Not marriage, and then courtship and love, but love, courtship, and marriage. The marriage service says that Isaac and Rebekah lived faithfully together, and this is a true record of their relationship. The eager, impulsive, affectionate, and daring nature of Rebekah was well adapted to the quiet, meditative, and retiring disposition of Isaac.

The Wrong Girl

But our last view of the home of Isaac and Rebekah is not an altogether pleasant one. Rebeka, in some strange way, had her strong affections diverted from a natural channel, which took in both her sons, Esau and Jacob, to one which embraced Jacob alone. Her whole heart and soul were set on the preferment of Jacob. It is true that, at the birth of the twins, it was told Rebekah that the elder should serve the younger. Moreover, Esau, when he was forty years old, married a woman of the land of Canaan, which was a grief of mind unto Isaac, but especially to Rebekah; and all credit to her for that. She said: "I am weary of my life because of the daughters of Heth.

If Jacob take a wife of the daughters of Heth, what good shall my life do me?"

In that mother's lament and dread we hear the echo of many a mother's voice. Few men marry women who altogether satisfy either their mothers or their sisters, for woman judges woman by herself. It was more of a blow to Rebekah to have Esau take a wife of the daughters of Heth than it would be to a mother today to have a son marry out of his rank and class. The great promises of the future were linked with her offspring, and now that Esau had apostatized, she is doubly anxious to keep Jacob from contamination and to see that he is properly married. The ill-favored plot which she invents and works out for the deception of Isaac, so that Jacob gets the blessing of the older son, must be considered in the light of this fact. It was not merely maternal ambition and pride, but religious hopes which animated her.

Love at First Sight

Having tricked his brother into selling the birthright, and then deceiving his father into giving him the blessing which belonged to Esau, Jacob had to flee the country. The first memorable incident on the exile's journey was his wonderful dream at Bethel, when he saw a ladder set up on earth, the top of which reached to heaven, and down which and up which went the angels of God. Fortified by this vision, Jacob made his way to what was then the far East, Mesopotamia. One day, far in the distance, Jacob, the lonely fugitive, saw three white dots on the horizon. Being of shepherd folk, he knew that these white dots were three flocks of sheep, and that near the sheep there must be a well and a habitation of men. At this his courage revives, and quickening his step he arrives at the well, where the three flocks are resting, waiting to be watered.

Jacob greets the shepherds as brethren, and he says, "Whence be ye?" They answer, "Of Haran are we." "Know ye Laban, the son of Nahor?" Jacob asked; and they answered: "We know him. He is well; and behold, Rachel, his daughter, cometh with the sheep." Jacob turned and looked upon Rachel, and in that glance was contained the whole future history of Jacob and the people of Israel.

The Bible, without any mawkishness or apology, frankly recognizes the power and influence of woman's beauty, and tells us in the case of both Rebekah and Rachel that they were fair to look upon. So fair was Rachel that with impulsive Jacob it was love at the first sight; and as we shall see, not only the first sight, but the second and the third, and on to the very end, until when, but a little way to Ephrath, where she had given him the second son, Rachel died and was buried, but never forgotten.

Jacob, inspired by his first glance, ran to the well, and, although it was something more than one man's job, because love had multiplied his powers, himself rolled away the great stone from the well and drew water for the flock of Rachel. That was a good start for Jacob. Chivalry and gallantry at the well won for Moses his bride. At this Mesopotamian well it helped Jacob to win the beautiful Rachel, and by many a well of life the chivalry which comes from the heart and expresses itself in kindness and in courtesy has commended man to woman.

Too often this sort of chivalry does not long survive the bridal day and withers under the hot sun of adversity and trial and sickness and daily contact of personalities. But in the case of Jacob, this beautiful chivalry endured to the end, and even the memory of Rachel is sacred to Jacob. This strong man, Jacob, had in him much that was sensual and abominable, together with much that was spiritual and noble, and it was fortunate for him that his heart settled on a woman like Rachel.

The Course of True Love

Jacob never did anything in a halfway fashion. He concluded this first act of their drama by kissing Rachel, and thus sealing their affection. Meanwhile, Rachel's father, Laban, came out and invited him into the house. He is not now the generous man whom we saw as a youth and as the brother of Rebekah. He makes a hard bargain with his nephew, Jacob, and practically sells his daughter, Rachel, to Jacob for seven years of hard labor.

There was another sister, Leah, not so attractive as the well-favored Rachel, and Jacob had no leanings in that direction. But he was glad to sign an agreement to labor seven years for the hand of Rachel. That would seem a long time to the people of our day and generation, who so often marry in haste and repent at leisure. Long betrothals of this sort ill suit the habits and thoughts of the world today, and, perhaps as a rule, are not to be desired, although, indeed, they have one advantage—that they afford opportunity for a complete acquaintance and a manifestation of both desirable and not so desirable traits and characteristics.

The course of true love never runs smooth. This saying is as true as it is ancient. Jacob found it to be so. Seven years must have seemed a dreadfully long time to him, and to Rachel, also, though, no doubt, living in the same encampment, they saw much of one another and took plenty of time to water the sheep at her father's well. Then comes the sentence, which makes this story immortal: "And Jacob served seven years for Rachel, and they seemed to him but a few days for the love he had for her."

Ambition, greed, hate—all these will make the day a week, and the week a year. Love is the great reducer and diminisher. So the years passed, and passed as if they were days. This is the kind of love that hopes all things and believes all things and endures all things; and those who have hardship, sickness, poverty, and yet with all this can carry a lantern of mutual love, are to be envied by those who have rank, station, talents, money, comforts; but no love or affection.

Retribution and Love's Labor Lost

At length the seven years are over, and the nuptial day so long awaited has arrived. The ceremonies appropriate to the occasion have been finished. Rachel's nurse, like the nurse of Rebekah, conducts her, closely veiled, to the tent of Jacob and retires. The veil is unwound, and lo! it is the face, not of Rachel, but the ill-favored Leah. Jacob's scorn of Leah is easy to understand. What is not so easy to understand at first is the unprotesting manner in which

Jacob acquiesces in this disgraceful fraud. Why was this? It must have been the reaction of his own conscience, "Whatsoever evil thing a man doeth, that also shall he receive again." And Jacob was paid in his own coin. He had deceived his own father, cheated his own brother. Now, in the tenderest and most sensitive area of his own life, he is cruelly deceived. "Whatsoever a man soweth, that shall he also reap."

We wonder that Jacob did not knock Laban down with his shepherd's staff, gather Rachel in his arms, put her on one of his camels, and elope westward. But the age of elopement had not yet come. So Jacob settled down to another term of service. It is not quite clear from the record whether he actually served another seven years for Rachel, or whether at the end of the week of nuptial celebrations over the marriage with Leah, he was married to Rachel, and then served another seven years. But whether married or not, he did serve fourteen years for the hand of Rachel and never regretted it. His was the love celebrated in the Song of Songs: "Many waters cannot quench love; neither can the floods drown it. If a man will give all the substance of his house for love, he would utterly be condemned."

Hope Deferred

After the marriage, Rachel, whose cry was, "Give me a child or I die," had to wait for a child almost as long as Jacob had to wait for her. This singular fact, not only in the case of Rachel, but in the case of almost every notable woman in the Scriptures, must have a deep significance. It was so in the case of Sarah; it was so in the case of the mother of Samson; it was so in the case of Hannah, the mother of Samuel; it was so in the case of Rebekah, and of the Shunammite woman; and of Elisabeth, the mother of John the Baptist. What is the meaning of this reiterated record of disappointment and hope deferred? It must be nothing less than to teach us that God wants above all else in His children faith. Faith is life's best child. It also emphasizes the fact that life is a discipline and a probation, even life in its tenderest and most intimate relationships.

And with the Morn Those Angel Faces Smile

But at length Rachel's period of waiting was over. First Joseph was born, and then, long after, when Jacob had returned to his own country, not far from Ephrath, the second son, Benjamin, was born. With this second son, Rachel gave her life and was buried. Jacob set up a pillar upon her grave. He could never forget that day, and long afterwards, when he was about to bless the sons of Joseph, the old man can remember the very spot where she died, and how far it was from Ephrath, for he says: "When I came from Padan, Rachel died by me in the land of Canaan, in the way, when yet there was yet a little way to come to Ephrath; and I buried her there in the way of Ephrath." Ephrath was Bethlehem; and where ages later another mother was to bring forth Jacob's mighty descendant, there Rachel's child was born.

The love of Jacob and his whole life henceforth centered in the two sons of Rachel. When he looked on the face of his youngest son, Benjamin, or when he saw Jacob's coat of many colors flashing in the sunlight, or, on a darker day, all torn and spotted with blood, when Joseph's cruel brothers held it up before his father, the one of whom Jacob was thinking was Rachel. When he came to die, Jacob said, "Few and evil have been my days." Life had been full of trouble and sorrow for Jacob. Yet his path had been lighted by the lamp of a wonderful affection, and to his dying day, Jacob, in the reverie of age, was again a youth in far-off Mesopotamia. Again he saw the three flocks of sheep like snow on the face of the desert; and once again by the well he saw the face that was even more wonderful to him than the golden ladder which in his dream at Bethel he had seen let down from heaven.

The Parent's and Pastor's Joy

Charles Haddon Spurgeon (1834-1892) is undoubtedly
the most famous minister of modern times. Converted in
1850, he united with the Baptists and soon began to preach
in various places. He became pastor of the Baptist church
in Waterbeach in 1851, and three years later he was
called to the decaying Park Street Church, London. Within a short time, the work began to prosper, a new church
was built and dedicated in 1861, and Spurgeon became
London's most popular preacher. In 1855, he began to
publish his sermons weekly; and today they make up the
fifty-seven volumes of *The Metropolitan Tabernacle Pulpit.* He founded a pastor's college and several orphanages.

This sermon is taken from *The Metropolitan Tabernacle Pulpit*, volume 19.

Charles Haddon Spurgeon

8

THE PARENT'S AND PASTOR'S JOY

I have no greater joy than to hear that my children walk in truth (3 John 4).

JOHN SPEAKS OF himself as though he were a father, and, therefore, we concede to parents the right to use the language of the text. Sure am I that many of you here present, both mothers and fathers, can truly say, "We have no greater joy than to hear that our children walk in truth." But John was not after the flesh the father of those of whom he was writing; he was their spiritual father; it was through his ministry that they had been brought into the new life; his relationship to them was that he had been the instrument of their conversion and had afterwards displayed a father's care in supplying them with heavenly food and gracious teaching. Therefore, this morning, after we have used the words as the expression of parents, we must take them back again and use them as the truthful utterance of all real pastors, "We have no greater joy than to hear that our children walk in truth."

The Parents' Joy

I. First, then, one of the parent's highest joys is his children's walking in truth; he has no greater joy. And here we must begin with the remark that it is *a joy peculiar to Christian fathers and mothers*. No parents can say from their hearts, "We have no greater joy than to hear that our children walk in truth," unless they are themselves walking in truth. No wolf prays for its offspring to become a sheep. The ungodly man sets small store by the godliness of his children, since he thinks nothing of it for himself. He who does not value his own soul is not likely to value the souls of his descendants. He who rejects Christ on his own account is not likely to be enamored of Him on his children's behalf. Abraham prayed for Ishmael, but I never read that Ishmael prayed for his son Nebajoth. I fear that many, even among professors of religion, could not truthfully repeat my text; they look for other joy in their children and care little whether they are walking in truth or not. They joy in them if they are healthy in body, but they are not saddened though the leprosy of sin remains upon them. They joy in their comely looks and do not inquire whether they have found favor in the sight of the Lord. Put the girl's feet in silver slippers, and many heads of families would never raise the question as to whether she walked the broad or the narrow road.

It is very grievous to see how some professedly Christian parents are satisfied so long as their children display cleverness in learning, or sharpness in business, although they show no signs of a renewed nature. If they pass their examinations with credit and promise to be well fitted for the world's battle, their parents forget that there is a superior conflict, involving a higher crown, for which the child will need to be fitted by divine grace and armed with the whole armor of God. Alas, if our children lose the crown of life, it will be but a small consolation that they have won the laurels of literature or art. Many who ought to know better think themselves superlatively blessed in their children if they become rich, if they marry well, if they strike out into profitable enterprises in trade, or if they attain eminence in the profession which they have espoused. Their parents will go to their beds rejoicing and awake perfectly satisfied, though their boys are hastening down to hell, if they are also making money by the bushel. They have no greater joy than that their children are having their portion in this life and laying up treasure where rust corrupts it. Though neither their sons nor daughters show any signs of the new birth, give no evidence of being rich toward God, manifest no traces of electing love or redeeming grace or the regenerating power of the Holy Spirit, yet there are parents who are content with their condition.

Now, I can only say of such professing parents that they have need to question whether they be Christians at all, and if they will not question it themselves, they must give some of us leave to hold it in serious debate. When a man's heart is really right with God, and he himself has been saved from the wrath to come and is living in the light of his heavenly Father's countenance, it is certain that he is anxious about his children's souls, prizes their immortal natures, and feels that nothing could give him greater joy than to hear that his children walk in truth. Judge yourselves, then, beloved, by the gentle but searching test of the text. If you are professing Christians but cannot say that you have no greater joy than the conversion of your children, you have reason to question whether you ought to have made such a profession at all.

Let us then remark, in the next place, that the joy which is mentioned in the text is *special in its object.* The expression is a thoughtful one. John did not write those words in a hurry but has compressed a great deal into them. He says, "I have no greater joy than to hear that my children walk in truth." Now, beloved parents, it is a very great joy to us if our children learn the truth. I hope you will not suffer one of them to grow up and leave your roof without knowing the doctrines of the gospel, without knowing the life of Christ and the great precepts of the Scripture, without having as clear an understanding as it is possible for you to give them of great principles and plan of salvation. When we perceive that our children, when we question them, thoroughly understand the gospel and are well rooted and grounded in its doctrines, it is a great joy to us, and well it may be. It is, however, far more a joy when those same children feel the truth; for, alas, we may know it and perish, unless we have felt its power within. Parent, was not your heart glad when you first saw the tear of repentance in the girl's eye? Did it not rejoice you when your son could say, "Father, I trust I have believed and am saved by the grace of God"? Yes, it is a greater joy that they should feel the power of truth than that they should know the letter of it. Such a joy I hope you will none of you be content to forego; it should be the holy ambition of every parent that all his house should be renewed of the Holy Spirit.

It is a great joy when our children avow their sense of the truth, when, knowing it and feeling it, they at last have the courage to say, "We would join with the people of God for we trust we belong to them." Oh, happy as a marriage day is that day in which the parent sees his child surrendered to the people of God, having first given his heart to the Christ of God! The baptism of our believing children is always a joyous occasion to us, and so it ought to be. Our parents before us magnified the Lord when they heard us say, "We are on the Lord's side," and we cannot but give thanks abundantly when the same privilege falls to us in the persons of our children.

But, beloved, there is anxiety about all this. When you teach your children, there is the fear that perhaps they will not learn to profit; when they feel, there is still the fear lest is should be mere feeling, and should be the work of nature and not the work of the Spirit of God; and even when they profess to be the Lord's, there yet remains the grave question, Will this profession last? Will they be able to stand to it and be true to the faith until life's latest hour?

But the joy of the text is higher than these three; though these have to come before it, and it grows out of them. "I have no greater joy than this, to hear that my children *walk* in truth." There is the point, their practical religion, their actual exemplification of the power of the gospel upon their lives. This proves that the teaching was well received, that the feeling was not mere excitement, that the profession was not a falsehood or a mistake, but was done in truth. What bliss it would be to us to see our sons grow up, and with integrity, prudence, uprightness, and grace, walk in truth, and to behold our daughters springing up in all their comeliness, lovely with the adornment of a meek and quiet spirit, becoming in their homes while with us, or in the new homes which speedily grow up around them, patterns of everything that is tender, gracious, and kind, and true. "I have no greater joy than this," says John, and truly all of you to whom such joy as this has been allotted can say, "Amen, Amen, it is even so." The joy before us has therefore a special possessor and a special object.

It is a healthful joy, beloved, in which we may indulge to the full without the slightest fear, for it is superior in its character to all earthly joys. "Not too much," is a good rule for everything which has to do with time; but this joy in our children's walking in the truth we may indulge in as much as we will; for, first, it is a spiritual joy, and therefore of a superior order. We do not joy to the full in the things which are seen of the eye and heard of the ear, for these are things of the flesh, which will decay; such as the garment which is eaten by the moth, and the metal which is devoured by the canker. We rejoice in the work of the Spirit of God, a work which will abide when this world shall have passed away. Hannah had some joy in the new coat which she made for young Samuel, but a far higher delight in the new heart which early showed itself in his actions. Our son promoted to be a king might cause us some delight; but to see our children made "princes in all the earth," according to that ancient promise, would be a diviner delight by far. Rejoice in it, then, without trembling, for spiritual joy will never intoxicate. Such joy arises from love to God and is therefore commendable. We love to see our children converted, because we love God. Out of love to Him, through His grace, we gave ourselves to Him, and now, in after years, the same love prompts us to present our children. As Barzillai in his old age prayed David to accept the personal service of his son Chimham, so would we, when our own strength declines, present our offspring to the Lord, that they may supply our lack of service. We have said—

> Had I ten thousand thousand tongues,
> Not one should silent be;
> Had I ten thousand thousand hearts,
> I'd give them all to thee.

Now as we have only one tongue of our own, we are intensely earnest that our children's tongues should sound forth the praises of the Savior. We have not another life on earth to call our own, but here are lives which the Lord has given us, and we are delighted that He should have them for Himself. We cry, "Lord, take this child's life and let it all be spent to thy service, from his earliest days till gray hairs shall adorn his brow." It is like the old soldier coming up to his king and saying, "I am worn out in thy service, but thou art so good a monarch that I have brought my son that he may serve thee from his youth up; let him take his father's place, and may he excel him in valor and in capacity to serve his king and country." Now, when our children walk in truth and love to God, it makes us rejoice that another heart is consecrated to His service.

We may well rejoice in the salvation and in the sanctification of our sons and daughters, because this is the way in which the kingdom of Christ is to be extended in the world. The hand which has held the standard aloft in the midst of the fury of war is at last palsied in death; happy is that standard-bearer who with expiring eye can see his own son springing forward to grasp that staff and keep the banner still floating above the host. Happy Abraham to be followed by an Isaac! Happy David to be succeeded by a Solomon! Happy Paul to have Timothy for a son! This is the apostolic succession in which we believe, and for which we pray.

How, in years to come, are we to see a seed of piety flourishing in the land, and the world conquered to Christ? How, indeed, but by means of the young men of Israel? We shall be sleeping beneath the green sward of the cemetery in peace; other voices will be heard in the midst of the assemblies of the saints, and other shoulders will bear the ark of the Lord through the wilderness. Where are our successors? Whence shall come these succeeding voices, and whence those needed shoulders of strength? We believe they will come from among our children, and if God grant it shall be so, we shall need no greater joy.

I will tell you why this is peculiarly the great joy of some Christian parents—it is because they have made it *a subject of importunate prayer.* That which comes to us by the gate of prayer comes into the house with music and dancing. If you have asked for it with tears, you will receive it with smiles. The joy of an answer to prayer is very much in proportion to the wrestling which went with the prayer. If you have felt sometimes as though your heart would break for your offspring unless they were soon converted to God, then, I will tell you, when they are converted you will feel as though your heart would break the other way, out of joy to think that they have been saved. Your eyes, which have been red with weeping over their youthful follies, will one day become bright with rejoicing over holy actions which will mark the work of the grace of God in their hearts. No wonder that Hannah sang so sweetly: for she had prayed so earnestly; the Lord had heard her, and the joy of the answer was increased by the former anguish of her prayer. We have no greater joy than this, that our children walk in truth; and it is a right and allowable joy, and springs from good sources, and we need not be afraid to indulge it.

This joy is quickening in its effect. All who have ever felt it know what an energy it puts into them. Those of you who have never yet received it, but are desiring it, will, I trust, be quickened by the desire. This is what it means. Is one son in the family converted to God? In that fact we rejoice, but we cannot linger over joy for one, we are impelled to think of the others. If God has been pleased to call half a household to salvation, there is a hunger and thirst in the parent's heart after this luscious delight, and that parent cries, "Lord, let them all be brought in, let not one be left behind." Are some of you so happy as to see all your children converted? I know some of you are. Oh, how holy and how heavenly ought your families to be when God has so favored you above many of His own people. Be very grateful, and while you are joyous, lay the crown of your joy at your Savior's feet; and if you have now a church in your house, maintain the ordinance of family worship with the greater zeal and holiness, and pray for others that the Lord in like manner may visit them also.

Beloved, have you some of your children converted while others remain unsaved? Then I charge you, let what the Lord has done for some encourage you concerning the rest. When you are on your knees in prayer say to your heavenly Father, "Lord, thou hast heard me for a part of my house, I beseech thee, therefore, to look in favor upon it all, for I cannot bear that any of my dear children should choose to remain thine enemies and pursue the road which leads to hell. Thou hast made me very glad with the full belief that a portion of my dear ones walk in the truth, but I am sad because I can see from the conduct of others that they have not yet been changed in heart and therefore do not keep thy statutes. Lord, let my whole household eat of the Paschal Lamb, and with me come out of Egypt, through thy grace."

I am sure, beloved, this is how you feel, for every true Christian longs to see all his children the called of the Lord. Suppose it could be put to us that one child of our family must be lost, and that we should be bound to make the dreadful choice of the one to be cast away, we should never bring ourselves to it, it would be too terrible a task; God will never appoint us such a misery. We have heard of a poor Irish family on shipboard, very numerous and very needy; a kind friend proposed to the father to give up entirely one of the little ones to be adopted and provided for. It was to be entirely given up, never to be seen again or in any way claimed as their own, and the parents were to make a selection. It is a long story, but you know how the discussion between the parents would proceed. Of course, they could not give up the eldest, for the simple reason that he was the firstborn. The second was so like the mother; the third was too weak and sickly to be without a mother's care. So the excuses went on and throughout the whole family, till they came to the last, and no one dared even to hint that the mother should be deprived of her darling. No child could be parted with; they would sooner starve together than renounce one.

Now, I am sure if the bare giving up of a child to be adopted by a kind friend would be a painful thing, and we could not come to a decision as to which to hand over, we could far less be able to surrender one beloved child to eternal destruction. God forbid we should dream of such a thing. We would cry day and night, "No, Lord, we cannot see them die. Spare them, we pray Thee!" We could almost rival the spirit of Moses: "Blot my name out of the book of life sooner than my children should be castaways.

Save them, Lord! save every one of them without exception, for thy mercy's sake!" We should make no differences in our prayers between one child and another.

Now, I am sure that we should be quite right in such desires and emotions, and very wrong if we were able to sit down and contemplate the eternal ruin of our own offspring with calm indifference. God has made you parents, and He does not expect you to act otherwise than as a parent's relations require you to act. That which would be unnatural cannot be right. As a Father Himself the Lord yearns over His erring children, and He can never be grieved with us if we do the same. Nowhere do you meet with rebukes of natural parental love unless it unwisely winks at sin. Even David's bitter lamentation, "O Absalom, my son, my son, would God I had died for thee. O Absalom, my son, my son!" is not censured by the Lord; neither do we find Him rebuking Abraham for saying, "O that Ishmael might live before thee!" These desires are so consistent with the natural instincts which He has Himself implanted, that, even if they are not always granted, they are never reprehended. Even if our child should turn out to be an Esau, or an Ishmael, or an Absalom, yet still the prayers of the father for him are not forbidden. How could they be?

Do not be afraid at any time when the pleading for the souls of your children; be importunate, be eager, be earnest, not for the child's life, that you must leave with God; not for the child's health, that also you may make a secondary matter; but for the child's soul. Stint not yourself in this, but wrestle as hard as you will, and say, "I will not let thee go except thou bless my children, every one of them! Their unregenerate state is my deepest sorrow: O Lord, be pleased to recover them therefrom."

Once more, this high joy of which we have spoken is *very solemn in its surroundings,* for it involves this alternative—"What if my children should not walk in truth?" Well, that means for us during this life many sorrows, nights of sleeplessness and days of anxiety. I have seen good men and great men crushed beneath the daily trouble caused by their children. "Children," said one, "are doubtful blessings," and he was near the truth. Blessings they are, and they can be made by God the choicest of blessings; but if they shall grow up to be dissolute, impure, ungodly, they will make our hearts ache.

> How sharper than a serpent's tooth it is
> To have a thankless child.

No cross is so heavy to carry as a living cross. Next to a woman who is bound to an ungodly husband, or a man who is unequally yoked with a graceless wife, I pity the father whose children are not walking in the truth, who yet is himself an earnest Christian. Must it always be so, that the father shall go to the house of God and his son to the alehouse? Shall the father sing the songs of Zion, and the son and daughter pour forth the ballads of Belial? Must we come to the communion table alone, and our children be separated from us? Must we go on the road to holiness and the way of peace, and behold our dearest ones traveling with the multitude the broad way, despising what we prize, rebelling against Him whom we adore? God grant it may not be so, but it is a very solemn reflection. More solemn still is the vision before us if we cast our eyes across the river of death into the eternity beyond. What if our children should not walk in the truth and should die unsaved? There cannot be tears in heaven; but if there might, the celestials would look over the bulwarks of the new Jerusalem and weep their fill at the sight of their children in the flames of hell, forever condemned, forever shut out from hope. What if those to whom we gave being should be weeping and gnashing their teeth in torment while we are beholding the face of our Father in heaven!

Remember the separation time must come. O you thoughtless youths! Between you and your parents there must come an eternal parting! Can you endure the thought of it? Perhaps your parents will first leave this world; oh, that their departure might touch your consciences and lead you to follow them to heaven! But if you go first, unforgiven, impenitent sinners, your parents will have a double woe in their hour.

How sadly have I marked the difference when I have gone to the funeral of different young people. I have been met by the mother who told me some sweet story about the girl, and what she did in life and what she said in death, and we have talked together before we have gone to the grave with a subdued sorrow which was near akin to joy, and I have not known whether to condole or to congratulate. But in other cases, when I have entered the house my mouth has been closed, I have asked few questions and very little has been communicated to me; I have scarcely dared to touch upon the matter. By-and-by the father has whispered to me, "The worst of all is, sir, we had no evidence of conversion. We would have gladly parted with the dear one if we might have had some token for good. It breaks my wife's heart, sir. Comfort her if you can." I have felt that I was a poor comforter, for to sorrow without hope is to sorrow indeed. I pray it may never be the lot of any one of us to weep over our grown up sons and daughters dead and twice dead. Better were it that they had never been born, better that they had perished like untimely fruit, than that they should live to dishonor their father's God and their mother's Savior, and then should die to receive, "Depart, ye cursed," from those very lips which to their parents will say, "Come, ye blessed of my Father, inherit the kingdom prepared for you." Proportionate to the greatness of the joy before us is the terror of the contrast. I pray devoutly that such an overwhelming calamity may never happen to any one connected with any of our families.

So far I have conceded the text to parents, now I am going to take it for myself and my brethren.

The Pastor's Joy

II. You may view, dear friends, the text as specifying the pastor's greatest reward. "I have no greater joy than to hear that my children walk in truth." The minister who is sent of God has spiritual children. They are as much his children as if they had literally been born in his house, for to their immortal nature he stands under God in the relationship of sire. It would seem we shall have but faint memories in heaven of earthly relationships, seeing they are there neither married nor given in marriage but are as the angels of God, and, therefore, the relationship of son and father will not exist in heaven, though I cannot but think that spirits which were grouped on earth will be associated in glory; but the duties and bonds of relationship will be ended. Relationships which relate to soul and spirit will last on. I may not look upon my sons in heaven as my children, but I shall recognize many of you as such, for it is through your soul or rather your new-born spirit, I am related to you. No minister ought to be at rest unless he sees that his ministry does bring forth fruit, and men and women are born unto God by the preaching of the Word. To this end we are sent to you, not to help you to spend your Sundays respectably, nor to quiet your consciences by conducting worship on your behalf. No, sirs, ministers are sent into the world for a higher purpose, and if your souls are not saved, we have labored in vain as far as you are concerned. If in the hands of God we are not made the means of your new birth, our sermons and instructions have been a mere waste of effort, and your hearing has been a mere waste of time to you, if not something worse. To see children born unto God, that is the grand thing. Hence every preacher longs to be able to talk about his spiritual sons and daughters. John did so.

Those who are the preacher's children are often known to him; they were to John, else he could not have spoken of them as "my children," and could not have had joy in them as his children. From this I draw the inference that it is the duty of everyone who receives spiritual benefit, and especially conversion, from any of God's servants, to let them know of it. John speaks about his children; but supposing there had been persons converted and John had never heard of it, suppose they had never made any profession, never joined the church. John might have lived and died without the comfort of knowing them, and without the joy of hearing that they walked in truth. Hence, permit me to remind some of you who, I trust, do know the Lord but have never confessed His name, that you do us grievous wrong. We have sought your good, and God has blessed us to you, and you deny us the fruit of our labor, which is that we should hear that God has owned our ministry in your consciences. Do not continue to defraud the laborer of his hire. You know how refreshing to the preacher is information that he has won a soul for Jesus. As cold water to a thirsty soul in a parching desert is such good news to us. I have had many such cups of water, but I am growing thirsty for more. I am grateful when the Lord works as He did only the other day, and I hear of it. I preached to you one morning a sermon to despairing souls. I said there might be few then present to whom it would apply. It was very grateful to me to find, a day or so after, that a friend from a considerable distance had been moved to come here that morning, and, after many years of despair, was brought into light and liberty through the sermon. Oh, how glad I felt! You cannot help preaching when you know that saving results follow. If God's Holy Spirit has blessed our word to you, do not refrain from acknowledging the blessing. Put on Christ publicly in baptism, according to His command; unite yourself with His church, and commune with the people among whom you have been born unto God.

It seems from our text that John was in the habit of hearing about his spiritual children: "I have no greater joy than *to hear*"—mark that—"than *to hear* that my children walk in the truth." That implies that, if you make a profession of your faith, people will talk about you. John could not have heard if others had not spoken. The man who makes a profession of religion, especially in a church like this, will be watched by all the world's eyes, and not by very friendly critics either. There are those at home, who know not the Savior, who, if they can find any fault in your character, will throw it at you, and say, "That is your religion, is it!" You will be men much spoken of, and reports of you will come to us; bad or good, we shall be sure to hear of them. We practice no spy system among the members of our church, and yet somehow or other in this large church of four thousand five hundred members, it very rarely happens that a gross act of inconsistency is long concealed. Birds of the air tell the matter. The eagle-eyed world acts as policeman for the church, and with no good intent becomes a watchdog over the sheep, barking furiously as soon as one goes astray.

I assure you, I have no greater joy than when I hear that the members of the church are walking in truth. When, for instance, a Christian young man dies, and his master writes to me, saying, "Have you got another member in your church like so-and-so? I never had such a servant before. I deplore his loss, and only wish I might find another of equally excellent character." Very different is our feeling when we hear it said, as we do sometimes, "I would sooner live with an ungodly man than with a professor of religion, for these professing Christians are a deal worse tempered, and more cantankerous than mere worldly people." Shame, shame on anybody who makes the world justly bring up so evil a report. Our joy is that there are others against whom no accusation can justly be brought.

You noticed that the apostle speaks of their "walk." The world could not report their private prayers and inward emotions. The world can only speak of what it sees and understands. So John heard of their "walk," their public character and deportment. Be careful, be careful of your private lives, my brethren, and I believe your public lives will be sure to be right; but remember that it is upon your public life that the verdict of the world will very much depend, therefore watch every step, action, and word lest you err in any measure from the truth.

What is it to "walk in truth"? It is not walking in *the* truth, or else some would suppose it meant that John was overjoyed because they were sound in doctrine and cared little for anything else. His joyous survey did include their orthodoxy in creed, but it reached far beyond. We will begin at that point and grant that it is a great joy to see our converts standing fast the essential, fundamental, cardinal truths of our holy faith. I rejoice that the nonsense of the so-called "modern thought" has no charms for you, you have not turned aside to doubt the deity of Christ, or the fall of man, or the substitutionary sacrifice, or the authenticity and inspiration of Scripture, or the prevalence of prayer. I am thankful that you hold fast the grand old doctrines of grace and refuse to exchange them for the intellectual moonshine so much in vogue just now. It is a great thing to hear of our people that they are abiding in the truth as they have been taught.

But to *walk in truth* means something more, it signifies action in consistency with truth. If you believe that you are fallen, walk in consistency with that truth, by watching your fallen nature and walking humbly with God. Do you believe that there is one God? Walk in that truth, and reverence Him and none beside. Do you believe in election? Prove that you are elect, walk in truth as the chosen, peculiar people of God, zealous for good works. Do you believe in redemption? Is that a fundamental truth with you? Walk in it, for "ye are not your own, ye are bought with a price." Do you believe in effectual calling and regeneration as the work of the Spirit of God? Then walk in the power of God, and let your holy lives prove that you have indeed been renewed by the supernatural work of God's grace. Walk in consistency with what you believe.

But walking in truth means yet more, it signifies "be real." Much of the walking to be seen in the world is a vain show, the masquerade of religion, the mimicry of godliness. In too many instances the man wears two faces under one hat and possesses a duplicate manhood; he is not real in anything good, he is a clever actor and no more. Alas, that one should have to say it, very much of the religiousness of this present age is nothing more than playing at religion. Why, look at the Christian year of the Ritualistic party in our national church, look at it, and tell me what is it? It is a kind of practical charade of which a sort of Passion-play is one act. The life of Christ is supposed to be acted over again, and we are asked to sing carols as if Jesus were just born, eat salt fish because He is fasting, carry palms because He is riding through Jerusalem, and actually to hear a bell toll His funeral knell as if He were dying. One day He is born, and another day He is circumcised, so that the year is spent in a solemn make-believe, for none of these things are happening, but the Lord Jesus sits in heaven, indignant thus to be made a play of. Have nothing to do with such things, leave the shadows and pursue the substance. Worship Christ as He is, and then you will regard Him as "the same yesterday, today, and forever." When men see you, let them see that what you believe you do believe in downright earnest, and that there is no sham about you. Then they will call you a bigot, for which be thankful; take the word home, keep it as an honorable title, far too good to be flung back upon your foe. They may call you a wild enthusiast, and in return pray God to make them enthusiastic too, for in such a cause one cannot be too much in earnest. Do not go through the world like respectable shades, haunting the tomb of a dead Christ, but be alive with the life of God, alive from head to foot to divine realities; to will you walk in truth. See how truly the apostles bore themselves; they were ready to die for the truth they held, and all their lives they were making sacrifices for it. Let your truthfulness be so powerful a force that others can see that you are carried away by its force and governed by its impulses. "I have no greater joy than this."

Why, when a preacher sees men thus walk in truth, may he make it his great joy? Because this is the end of our ministry, it is this we aim at. We do not live to convert people to this sect or that, but to holy living before God and honest dealing with men. This is the grand thing, and when we see this achieved, we have no greater joy. This is the design of the gospel itself. Christ loved His church and gave Himself for it, that He may present it to Himself, a perfect church, without spot or wrinkle or any such thing. A holy people are the reward of the Redeemer's passion, well may they be the joy of those friends of the Bridegroom who stand and rejoice greatly because the Bridegroom's joy is fulfilled. The holiness of Christians is the great means of spreading the gospel. Beyond all other missions I commend the mission of holiness.

They preach best for Christ who preach at the fireside, who preach in the shop, whose lives are sermons, who are themselves priests unto God, whose garments are vestments, and whose ordinary meals are sacraments. Give us a holy, consecrated people, and we will win, for these are the omnipotent legions with which the world shall be conquered to Christ. We joy in a holy people because they bring glory to God. Mere professors do not so; inconsistent professors dishonor God, of whom I tell you even weeping that they are the enemies of the cross of Christ. A people walking in truth crown the head of Jesus. They compel even blasphemers to hold their tongues, for when they see these holy men and women, they cannot say anything against the gospel which has produced such characters.

Beloved, if you love your pastor, if you love the Bible, if you love the gospel, if you love Christ, if you love God, be a holy people. You who profess to be saved, be true, be watchful. If you would not grieve us, if you would not dishonor the gospel, if you would not crucify Christ afresh and put Him to an open shame, walk as Christ would have you walk; abhor that which is evil, cleave to that which is good. Be in your speech and in your temper, in your business transactions with your fellowmen, and in your communications in the family circle, men approved of God, such as you will wish to have been when your Lord shall come, for He is at the door, and blessed are those servants who are ready for His coming.

If you are not what you ought to be, I beseech you do not make a profession; and if you have made a profession and have dishonored it, humble yourselves in the sight of God and go once more to the fountain filled with blood, for there is forgiveness and mercy for you still. Jesus will willingly receive you, even though you have done Him such despite. Return as a prodigal son to the father's house, and you shall find the fatlings killed for you and the best robe put upon you. As we are getting near the close of the year, earnestly pray that if anything in the time past has been evil, it may suffice us to have wrought the will of the flesh; and now, henceforth, in the new year may we live in newness of life and enjoy together the sweet privilege of hearing that our children walk in truth, while we ourselves, through grace, are walking in it too, and the church is built up and multiplied by the Spirit of truth. May the Lord bless you all, for Jesus Christ's sake.

The Heritage of Children

George Campbell Morgan (1863-1945) was the son of a British Baptist preacher, and he preached his first sermon when he was 13 years old. He had no formal training for the ministry, but his tireless devotion to the study of the Bible helped him to become one of the leading Bible teachers of his day. Rejected by the Methodists, he was ordained into the Congregational ministry. He was associated with Dwight L. Moody in the Northfield Bible conferences and as an itinerant Bible teacher. He is best known as the pastor of the Westminster Chapel, London (1904-17 and 1933-45). During his second term there, he had Dr. D. Martyn Lloyd-Jones as his associate. Morgan published more than 60 books and booklets, and his sermons are found in *The Westminster Pulpit* (London, Pickering and Inglis).

This sermon is from Volume 1 of *26 Sermons by G. Campbell Morgan*, published by The College Press, Joplin, Missouri, in "The Evangelical Reprint Library" series.

George Campbell Morgan

9

THE HERITAGE OF CHILDREN

Scripture Lesson: Psalms 126-128

Lo, children are an heritage of the Lord (Psalm 127:3).

THIS IS A PSALM of the home life. It is the central psalm of the songs of ascents. Immediately following that which is a complete psalter within itself (Psalm 119) in its setting forth of the perfections of the will of God, we have fifteen psalms, and each of them bears the title Song of Ascents. There is little doubt that these fifteen psalms also constitute a complete collection within themselves, and the editor of this great book of Hebrew devotional poetry incorporated the whole collection and placed it immediately after the psalm celebrating the perfections of the will of God.

At the center of these Songs of Ascents is this psalm of the home. I am quite familiar with the fact that there may be, and indeed is, difficulty in interpreting the meaning of this recurring title, Song of Ascents. There can be very little doubt, however, that they constituted a series of songs which were sung by pilgrims as they traveled up to Jerusalem for the celebration of feasts and worship, songs sung by pilgrims who had known the places of exile and of distance. If you follow the songs through you will approach it singing, as they come of the varied facts of the government of their one God Jehovah. Right at the center of the fifteen is this little Psalm 127, seven preceded it and seven follow it.

Glance back at the psalm immediately before this one, Psalm 126, and you find that it celebrates Jehovah as the Restorer of the pilgrim to his city and to his place of worship. Glance at the next one, Psalm 128, and you will find that it celebrates Jehovah as the Keeper of the home of the pilgrim; and that it moves in this sequence—the godly man, the godly home, the godly city, the godly nation. Between the psalm celebrating Jehovah as Restorer of the pilgrim, and the one celebrating Him as the Keeper of the home, is this psalm which celebrates Him as the Maker of the home. Notice in this psalm that the building of the home, the guarding of the city, and all the interests of toil within the city are preliminary matters. At the center of this central psalm you will find the words of my text, "Lo, children are an heritage of the Lord."

All this is not waste of time, especially for the young people. Fifteen psalms, songs of ascents, songs of pilgrims returning after exile to the city and government of God, the worship of God, and the ultimate realization of the high purpose of God. The central one celebrates the home life; the home is at the center. Of the central psalm the central verse is, "Lo, children are an heritage of the Lord."

Notice the things preliminary—the house built, the city guarded, toil crowned, all for the sake of the children.

> Except the Lord build the house,
> They labor in vain that build it;
> Except the Lord keep the city,
> The watchman waketh but in vain.
> It is vain for you that ye rise up early, and so late take
>   rest,
> And eat the bread of toil.

There is no need for anxiety in the matter of toil if you are in fellowship with Jehovah, "For so He giveth unto His beloved in sleep." Jehovah building the house; Jehovah guarding the city; Jehovah in fellowship with His people in their toil, the Partner Who never sleeps but carries on the work while we rest in the night, that we may enter into greater fullness of blessing in the morning. The house built by Jehovah, the city guarded by Jehovah, the work cooperated in by Jehovah, and all for the sake of the children. "Lo," the word arrests our attention. To this the Psalmist had been leading up, "Lo, children are an heritage of the Lord."

The Central Thought

Let us then leave the surrounding psalms, and, indeed, all of this psalm except its central declaration. Of course, it will be seen at once that the first application of this message is to parents. The first application of this central word of the great psalm is to the fathers and mothers of the children referred to. Yet let this also be remembered, that those are all included who for love of God and humanity are giving themselves in any way to the service of the children. "Children are an heritage of the Lord." It is a great word, which helps those of us who are parents to understand at once our privileges and our responsibilities. It has application also to all those who are caring for the children in any way in the schools, and our beloved friends who take care of these orphans are specially included. "Children are an heritage of the Lord." No life is complete which is uninfluenced by children. If there are not children in your own home, then in the name of God get out and help children somewhere else. Your own lives must lack the final touches and influences which make for perfection of character, unless somehow you are allowing these ministers of God to touch your lives; for as you help them you receive from them a sacred and hallowed ministry.

Let us examine the declaration and apply the same. First, "Children are an heritage." This is a somewhat peculiar and unusual word in this connection. We have no business to hurry over it as a sort of poetic figure of speech which may not have very much meaning in it. I maintain that though it is a peculiar word in this connection, it is fundamental. What is a heritage? Something devolving by right of inheritance. Something which is actually possessed, which is in itself wealth, something involving responsibility because it devolves by right of inheritance. "Children are an heritage." "Children are an heritage from the Lord." Let us start there. We inherit children from God, whether they are our own in the home life, or whether they are those to whom we are giving ourselves; we are to look upon them as an inheritance—I do not like my next word, I will come back to it presently—

as property, not absolute and final, but nevertheless wealth, an heritage. You remember George MacDonald's poem on "Baby." I give it to the children in passing in order that the adults may hear its final words:

Where did you come from, baby dear?
Out of the everywhere into here.

Where did you get those eyes so blue?
Out of the sky as I came through.

What makes the light in them sparkle and spin?
Some of the starry twinkles left in.

Where did you get that little tear?
I found it waiting when I got here.

What makes your forehead so smooth and high?
A soft hand stroked it as I went by.

What makes your cheek like a warm white rose?
I saw something better than anyone knows.

Whence that three-cornered smile of bliss?
Three angels gave me at once a kiss.

Where did you get this pearly ear?
God spoke, and it came out to hear.

Where did you get those arms and hands?
Love made itself into bonds and bands.

Feet, whence did you come, you darling things?
From the same box as the cherubs' wings.

How did they all just come to be you?
God thought about me, and so I grew.

But how did you come to us, you dear?
God thought about you, and so I am here.

That is the truth; God thinks about us, and so sends us the children, and they are "An heritage of the Lord."

What is the value of the possession? I want to use two words; and let the legal mind be patient with me. There are two words of which we often make use today, personalty and personality; we need them both if we are to understand this word heritage in this connection. "Children are an heritage of the Lord" constituting personalty and creating personality. In my use of the word personalty I do not mean realty, not real estate. Your children are not your real estate; they are God's real estate. You can make them yours upon certain conditions. They are personalty; they are things that belong to us, movable things in more senses than one. Some time ago, in a great temperance convention in one of the Western States in America, as the delegates assembled in the hall specially erected for the great gatherings, there hung in front of them, where everyone could see it as they came in, a banner on which was inscribed the words, "One boy is worth more to God than all the silver and gold in the world; and so he is to you, if he is your boy." The most valuable, the most precious property we have are our children.

If we could only get away from the idea of sermon preaching and listening this morning, and have a quiet, simple talk along these lines, we should be greatly helped.

The wealth of a little child. Physically, what flower is so beautiful, what diamond flashes with such luster? What is there in the world of art that compares with a little child physically? What fascination is there like the fascination of a little child mentally? What is there in this wide world so absolutely and charmingly entrancing as to watch the opening mind of a little child, and listen to its questions, observe its quaint conceits, and be rebuked over and over again by its unerring wisdom? The children in your home are your true wealth. By comparison with them all other things you possess are as nothing, and other things you lack matter nothing. "Children are an heritage of the Lord," the most sacred, wonderful and precious wealth that can ever come into human possession.

Yet take a step forward with me. They do more than constitute personalty; *they create personality*, calling forth in us all the highest things, if we will but let those highest things answer the call; compelling us, if we have anything of honesty within us, to say nothing of Christianity, to self-culture. I do not desire to state what I am now going to say dogmatically; I am talking out of my own heart and my own growing experience when I say that I often wonder if after all God does not mean children to train us, rather than mean us to train children. Is that a superlative way of stating it? Every father and mother knows exactly what I mean. We are responsible for these children, and, oh, what they do for us! That is what made me say if there are no children in your own home, get into contact with child-life somewhere; if nowhere else, then in the slums give yourself up to the children there. The children of the slums may also minister to your making as you minister to their making. Mark how they call forth the highest in us. A little child demands your faith, which is confidence in the child's ability. A child enkindles anew your hope, which is expectation of the child's realization. A little child simply storms you and demands your love. All these highest things are brought out by a little child creating personality—faith, hope, love. Children call for them and gain them whenever we listen to their call. Remember how they compel self-culture, and how they demand that you shall practice self-restraint. How they demand that you yourself shall never cease to grow, but by development of life shall be prepared for all they are asking of you. How they call forth ceaseless vigilance and activity so that all the greatest things of your life are brought into play and move toward perfection in the presence of children. "Children are an heritage of the Lord," constituting personalty, creating personality.

Let us go a step further. "An heritage of the Lord." "Of the Lord," not *from* the Lord, although that is included; but the idea is infinitely more than that. It is not only that God has sent children into our homes and into our cities, and that they belong to us. They are "an heritage of our Lord." He does not abandon His claim to the children. He still claims them as His own. No little child is the absolute property of any parent. Let me illustrate on a much lower level. You recognize that in the matter of nationality the State has long ago stepped in and said no child is the final property of any parent. No parent can do exactly what he likes with his child. The State will not allow you to ill-treat your child in the physical realm. The

State says, A boy born within these realms belongs first of all to the State. I know many of you are in rebellion against that in the region of the mental and the realm of the spiritual; perchance you may be right so to be. Nevertheless, the fact abides; the State has prior right in every little child. You can neither starve your child nor neglect your child's education. What is this action on the part of the State? It is a recognition, even though unconfined, perchance not perfectly understood, of that earliest right of all, the right of God in the little child. The powers that be are ordained of God, even though they are often forgetful of Him. He nevertheless does make even the wrath of men to praise Him, and the remainder He restrains. He is governing the affairs of men. Wherever you find that the light of Christianity has come, and the influence of the Christ-gospel has permeated society and touched legislation, you will find the right of the child has been recognized. I will put that so superlatively as to say this, you may trace the upward march of nations by their relation to a little child. You may trace the downward career of nations by the self-same method. Wherever the State puts a little child in the midst, thinks of the child, cares for the child, legislates for the child, the State is ensuring its own well-being. Insisting upon the fact that the child is not finally the property of father or mother, the State is accepting beneficent responsibility.

Let us leave that lower level of consideration and climb to the higher. There is no passage in all this wonderful Divine library which to my own mind more powerfully sets forth the fact I am attempting to emphasize than an almost incidental word, but none the less powerful, in the letter to the Hebrews. You will remember the writer of that letter says: "We had the fathers of our flesh to chasten us, and we gave them reverence. Shall we not much rather be in subjection unto the Father of spirits, and live?" (Heb. 12:9). Notice the contrast—fathers of the flesh, the Father of spirits. I am but the father of my children after the flesh. God is the Father of my children so far as spiritual life is concerned.

Generation of spiritual being is not in the hands of men; it is an act of God. He retains this final, ultimate claim upon all our children. They are an heritage, wealth in very deed; but they are of the Lord, and therefore we are responsible to God for them. Children are His freehold, His real estate. They are our leasehold, our personalty. We may possess the freehold if we will. We may not do what we like with our children. If the State declares that we may not do what we like with them physically or mentally now, God stands at the back of the State and declares that we have no right to do what we choose to do with them physically, mentally, or spiritually.

We are laying up for ourselves severe reckonings with God Almighty if we are feeding our children, educating them, and starving their spiritual life. Unless we also recognize that the main, essential thing in a little child is its kinship to God and its relation to God, and recognize our responsibility for our children as His creation, our leasehold, then when He comes to deal with us in that mystic and wonderful country that lies beyond our ken—let no word of mine describe what will happen, but let every father and mother ponder the grave responsibility of dealing with these children as though they were dust alone, or mind only, forgetting that the essential fact which flashes through the blue or brown eye of every girl and boy is that of relation to God, and that the children in our own homes are not ours finally, but His. That is the supreme truth. We rejoice in the great heritage; and what a heritage it is, the mystery of love and the mystery of laughter! We thank God for them all our days, but they belong not ultimately to us in this probationary life, but to God Himself. We are responsible to Him for them.

Possession and Appreciation

Secondly, therefore, that which is the necessary outcome of such consideration, the application of the declaration. The law of possession of our heritage is that of the power of appreciation of the heritage. That is always so. You may have as yours in some material property sense, a thing you never possess. A blind man may be the owner of pictures, but he cannot possess them. To appreciate pictures you need sight, and not sight alone, but artistic sight, capacity for entering into all their mystic value.

It is equally so with books. You can furnish your library with shelves and fill them with books, yet never possess your books; buy them, pay for them, subscribe for them, but you do not possess them. You possess your books by the power of being able to appreciate them.

So also with your lands. You may own broad acres and never possess them. You may own them, hunt over them, shoot over them in the proper season, but never possess them. You say, They are mine; but they are not yours unless you have entered into the true spirit of them. Many a man with half an acre of garden, who knows how to touch every blade of grass and to labor in cooperation with God, possesses more land than the man who owns broad acres.

Let us leave that realm of illustration. How am I to enter into possession of my children? The law of possession is the power of appreciation. Two things are necessary for appreciation of children. First, fellowship with the Father; secondly, true sympathy with the child. Does that first statement of mine seem almost startling, appalling to some of you? To appreciate my children, I must enter into fellowship with the Father. I affirm it most resolutely. Children; the very name suggests fatherhood. Fatherhood; what is it? Sometimes we say that God has taken our name father in order to teach us what He is. That is not a correct statement. God has lent us His name Father in order to teach us what we ought to be.

How am I to know what I ought to be? Only as I know God, and know what He is, and enter into fellowship with God in His estimate of the value of the child, in His enterprise for the child, in His purpose for the child. How can these things be? All these things have been revealed to us in His Son Jesus Christ. I do not want to hide by multiplicity of words the thing that is in my heart. You cannot properly deal with children unless you are godly men and women. You can do a great deal for them, but you can never possess them. They will never be anything more than personalty. They will never become real possessions of yours.

I speak with grave solemnity; I do not want to possess my children only for the little while of this life, but to hold them forever. God keeps to Himself the final possession of my children, and I can only enter into that freehold of my children as I come into fellowship with God. That is the whole argument here. Fellowship with the Father. My dear Sir, if you have so lost your vision of high and noble things that you care very little for God and godliness, in the name of God look into the faces of your children once again, and if not for your own sake, for their sakes, that they may enter into life, that you may possess them forever, come into fellowship with God Himself.

Involved in that is the other fact, that there must be sympathy with the child. Not patronage, but sympathy. You will never possess your own children by patronizing them, and certainly never the children in the Sunday School by patronizing them. Sympathy; that is, not sitting down by the side of a child and saying you sympathize with it, that may be the gravest mistake; but sympathy of spirit. If I am to possess my child I must be a child; the mind open, the heart tender, the will yielding to control. When my mind becomes locked and sealed and I have no eastern window, I shall fail to appeal to children. When my heart is hard and lacks emotion and tenderness, I shall be losing them. They will drift away from me. They may remain within the sphere of my moral influence and respect me, but I shall not hold them. When my will is no longer open to control, when it is so strong that I insist they obey it because it is my will, I lose them. Unless I am prepared to show them there is reason in my will and that the impulse of the will which I desire they should yield to for the while is that higher Will, the impulse of which is love for them, unless these things are so, we shall lose our children.

The Lord made no mistake when into the midst of office-seeking disciples He put a child. That is the type, "Except ye turn, and become as little children, ye shall in no wise enter into the Kingdom of heaven." The ancient Scriptures made no mistake when they declared, through the seers looking on to the ultimate day of the establishment of the Kingdom of God, "A little child shall lead them." You know how true that is. I wish you had been here last night. I would have shown you a demonstration of it that you would never have forgotten. We had our gymnastic display, and the person who captured the whole audience was a wee bit lassie four years old, skipping! We caught her in our arms and kissed her. I am not sure it was good for her; still, the little child held us, captured us. The most hopeful sign about that assembly was that there was enough childhood in their hearts to make them love that child. The law of possession is that of the power of appreciation.

Hear that which is the necessary deduction from this consideration. Outside these conditions of fellowship with God and sympathy with the child, the heritage is forfeit. God never gives up His right. To share it we must enter into fellowship, partnership with Him. We do not lose our children by death. We lose them in life. There are some things a man cannot preach about any further; he has to be silent. What grave responsibilities come surging, thundering upon his own heart! I have not lost the child He has taken to be with Himself. We lose them here.

Children constitute the supreme heritage of humanity in these days of humanity's training and probation. The most precious possession of England, what is it? The children. London's wealth, what is it? The children; I do not care whether they live in the East or the West, children are children. The most precious things in your home today are the children. The most precious things in your life, Sunday School teacher, are those children you gather about you on Sunday.

Therefore everything should be done in the interest of the children. The house should be built for the children, and furnished for the children, arranged for the children. I will whisper this in an aside; if in your house there is no room in which the children can play except that best room, sweep the fancy furniture out, and give the children a chance. The thing that threatens England today is the breakup of home life. We have to get back to make home *home* for the children; everything should be made to gather about the little child. The house built, the city kept, toil undertaken all on behalf of the children. I do not think there is anything more plaintive in all this Divine library, more full of agony than a word out of the Old Testament, a word that came sighing and sobbing over the lips of poor old Jacob, "If I be bereaved of my children, I am bereaved" (Gen. 42:36). Yes, but some of you are bereaving yourselves of your children. Some of you businessmen hardly ever see them. A deacon of mine—not in this church, not in London—once said to me, with a sort of smile of amusement: "Do you know, I have not seen my children, except when they have been asleep, for a month." It was on a Sunday morning, after the service. I asked him what he meant, and he replied: "I am so busy just now; I am off in the morning before they are awake, and when I get back at night they are asleep." I said to him: "Don't you dare to come here and worship tonight; you stay at home with your bairns, or you will be bereft of your children."

I call you back, you fathers and mothers, to the children—to God's children, that most gracious heritage of all—in order that you may find them and possess them. I call you to fellowship with the Father. Now do you see the value of Christ's words, "Ye must be born again"? Born again that I may be a child and get hold of my own children. Back through the sacred ministry of the Holy Spirit, taking away the heart of stone and giving the heart of flesh, clearing away the mists and giving me true vision of God, of my own children; back through the new birth into new possession of the children! I call you to the Divine heritage of your children through the Divine life which is yours, as you are a child of God. May He give us to see the value, to understand the responsibilities, to dedicate ourselves anew to fulfillment, for "Children are an heritage of the Lord."

NOTES

Christic and the Home

George H. Morrison (1866-1928) assisted the great Alexander Whyte in Edinburgh, pastored two churches, and then became pastor in 1902 of the distinguished Wellington Church on University Avenue in Glasgow. His preaching drew great crowds; in fact, people had to line up an hour before the services to be sure to get seats in the large auditorium. Morrison was a master of imagination in preaching, yet his messages are solidly biblical. From his many published volumes of sermons, I have chosen this message, found in *The Wind on the Heath*, published in 1931 by Hodder and Stoughton, London, and republished by Kregel Publications in 1993.

George H. Morrison

10

CHRIST AND THE HOME:
A CHRISTMAS MEDITATION

THERE ARE TWO thoughts which meet and mingle when we gather together at a Christmas season. The one is the thought of Jesus Christ, and the other is the thought of home. The very name that we give to this happy time has Christ for its first and most important syllable—this is not Candlemas nor Marymas; this is *Christ*mas. And then the manger and the swaddling clothes and the newborn infant and the mother, all these speak to us of home. We have seasons when we associate Christ with heaven; we have Easter Sunday and Whitsunday. But at Christmas— though it be full of heaven—it is natural to associate Christ with home. And so tonight we shall think of Christ a little in His connection with the life of home, the sweetest and tenderest of all relationships.

How deeply Christ had been influenced by His home is apparent to every reader of the Gospels. Through all His life and ministry and death the music of home rings like a sweet refrain. As life goes on, and the years unfold their chronicle, we all discover that home has been determinative. We never escape it. It is always with us. It tells to our dying hour in weal or woe. That is why every biography begins, not with the hour of effort or achievement, but with the father's stock, and with the mother's ancestry, and with the environment of infant days.

A man may travel to the far Antipodes, or he may rise to be the friend of princes; but there are two things which he never leaves behind when he takes the wings of morning or mounts with wings as eagles. One is the fore-ordering will of God, Who sees the end from the beginning, and the other is the influence of home. Like a

127

sweet fragrance or a clammy vapor it clings to his garments till his dying hour. Like some fine tonic or some insidious poison it courses in his blood with every heartbeat. And therefore the irreparable loss in life when homes are foolish, worldly, uninspiring, when motherhood suggests no lovely things, when fatherhood recalls no comradeship.

How Christ Felt the Influence of the Home

This influence of home, felt by us all, was felt in its full intensity by Christ. In His words and deeds—in His life and in His death—"home sweet home" is like a sweet refrain. The first miracle He ever wrought was wrought in a home and at a marriage feast. The most beautiful parable He ever uttered was about a son who was a prodigal. The richest and deepest name He had for God was drawn from the tender relationships of home—"Our *Father* which art in heaven." This Man spoke as never man spoke: He spoke as many of us would be ashamed to speak. We speak of tendencies and of environment. He spoke of little children in the marketplace. He spoke of a woman sweeping out a cottage, and of another baking in the kitchen, and of a father who was brokenhearted as he thought of a prodigal son in a far country.

Like a great wave the thought of home broke over Him when He saw a widow mourning for her child. He called to His aid the mighty power of heaven just to give her back her son again. And all this shows that in the thought of Christ such simple words as son and child and mother were infinitely precious and important.

Somehow or other, then, right through the life of Jesus you feel the power and influence of home. It colors His language. It inspires His miracles. It kindles His passion and directs His vision. Even amid the agonies of Calvary and in the hour of excruciating pain the old familiar music is not silent.

The Melody of a Happy Home

Well now, I want you to think about where that melody of home was born. It was not born in the high expanse of heaven. It was born in the lowly home at Nazareth. There are men and women whom we sometimes meet who irresistibly suggest to us that their home was beautiful. There is a touch which nothing else can give that tells of a beautiful and reverential childhood. And that man must be blind as any Cyclops after Odysseus had wrought his havoc, who does not recognize that touch in Christ. We talk of the silent years at Nazareth. They are only silent because we make them so. There is music enough to spare waiting to fill them, out of the oratorio that follows. The evangelists were too wise to go to Nazareth to interrogate some patriarchal villager; they said, Do you want to know about Christ's home? Study His ministry and find it there. What could the gossips in Nazareth have known?—the best and most beautiful homes have no history. It is when homes are unhappy and when parents quarrel that the neighbors are able to satisfy the chronicler. The most beautiful homes are always quiet homes and leave no record in any village gossip. Their only record is the children's lives, when duty calls and when the battle comes. We talk and sing of the fair green hills of Nazareth, and I have no doubt these hills were very fair. But judging by the years which are preserved for us, there was one thing at Nazareth fairer still to Christ. It was the home where as a boy He played, and watched His mother tidying and baking, and heard her singing, when the day was over, of "old unhappy far-off things."

One would observe in passing that from the Gospel record it is clear that Christ was never ashamed of home. There are sons and daughters who are ashamed of home, and of their fathers and their mothers also. It was a very old-fashioned home, that home at Nazareth. It was a home of sweet and simple piety. It had caught no polish from the Roman empire; Joseph was but a humble working man. It was a home like countless homes in Scotland, whose only adornment is the fear of God, but which have sent out sons to teach and preach and heal, or to govern the millions of India.

It is not such sons who are ever ashamed of home. They honor their father and their mother. They come back to the cottage from their Indian palace and are proud to call that bent old woman mother. The kind of children who are ashamed of home, and of a father who has never learned his manners, are the children whose infinitely little world is their infinitely little selves. Think of it, Christ was the King of kings, and yet He never was ashamed of Nazareth; never despised it—never once ignored it—never blushed at being the carpenter's son. And if ever you have been tempted so—and I know not how you have been tempted—I want you to put it right this Christmas Sunday.

The Temptations of Home

It is clear also from the Gospel narrative that Christ knew the temptations of the home. The words of Christ that have the harshest ring in them are the words He spoke to those who loved Him most. To the sinner Christ was infinitely pitiful. A bruised reed He would not break. Even with Judas there is the note of gentleness: *"Friend, wherefore are thou come?"* But sometimes in the hour of fierce temptation there is a violent recoil that looks like harshness and that is only found with those who loved Him.

There was one who loved Him more than any other. It was the mother who had cradled Him. With all the wonderful tenderness of motherhood she clung in yearning love to her firstborn. And when the Spirit of God came down on Him at Jordan, and He was driven from home into the wilderness, it was like a dagger in His mother's heart.

The eternal mystery of love is this, that it holds within its breast a twofold craving—the craving to give and to give everything, and also the quenchless craving to possess. You have them both in the perfect love of God, which gives to the uttermost, yet wants us always; and you have them both in the mother-love of Mary. She could not release her hold upon her child. She wanted Him, and wanted Him at home. It was breaking her heart that He should run such risks and fling a defiance that must end in death. And so she sought Him, and tried to interfere with Him, and wanted Him back in the quiet peace of Nazareth, and to Christ that was a terrible temptation.

The worst temptations do not come from enemies—the worst temptations come from those who love us; from those who would lay their lives down for us gladly, and yet have never heard our calling voices; from those to whom we have to say sometimes, as the poet said on going to the wars, "I could not love thee, dear, so much, loved I not honor more."

There comes a time in many a man's life when the thought of home must take a second place. Visions are beckoning—there is the call of God—conscience is crying and will not be denied. And there can be no question that our blessed Lord felt that temptation in its full intensity, for he was tempted in all points like as we are. When you are tempted in such ways as that, remember that Jesus understands when you are tempted by dear human love to be a traitor to the call of God. It is Nazareth, the love of Mary, which gives their infinite pathos to these words, "Whoso loveth father or mother more than me is not worthy of me."

There was one trial at home which Jesus knew, and which it is well we too should remember. He not only knew what it was to be loved at home; He knew what it was to be misunderstood at home. There was a period in the life of Principal Rainy when he was exposed to violent abuse. Hardly a day passed but in the newspapers his actions were misrepresented and distorted. And one day, in Melville Street in Edinburgh, Dr. Whyte met him. "Rainy," he said, "I can't understand you, you seem as radiant and blissful as a child." And Dr. Rainy answered very quietly, "Ah, but Whyte, *I'm very happy at home.*" When a man is happy at home he can face anything. Even the newspaper has not terrors. It is not the misunderstanding of the public that weighs a straw with men whose hearts are pure. But one of the sorest trials of human life, especially where life is young and ardent, is to be misunderstood *at home.*

To get no sympathy within the home—to have no one there who really understands—to find all natural utterance repressed—to hear the cherished ideal being sneered at, for sensitive impressionable youth there are few things harder in life to bear than that, and such was the experience of Jesus. Many believed in Him, let us be thankful. But none of His brothers, we are told, believed in Him. Like Joseph's brethren, when he came home at night they would say, "Behold, this dreamer cometh." And how that must have weighed upon the Lord in the eager delicate beauty of His youth, I leave with you to try to realize.

Do I speak to any who are all alone at home? Who find no sympathy from brother or from sister? To any who would never dream of uttering at home all that is deepest in their hearts? My lonely hearer, in the home at Nazareth, and right on to the hour of resurrection, remember that our Lord had that to bear.

The Burden of the Home

I close by suggesting to you another thought, that Jesus bore the *burden* of the home. For it is commonly held, and held, I think, with truth, that Joseph died while our Lord was still in boyhood. The last time that we hear of Joseph is when they went up to Jerusalem together. After that we always hear of Mary; after that we never hear of Joseph. Just when the crisis of the child had come, just when He heard the calling of the world, He had to go home again, and take the burden up, and support the household as a carpenter. "Wist ye not I must be about my Father's business?" That tells you what was surging in His heart. He had been dreaming of kingdoms in these quiet days, or the devil would never have tempted Him with kingdoms. Then Joseph died, and Mary was a widow, and the younger children must have bread to eat—and the Lord became the carpenter of Nazareth. For long years out of the thirty-three, King of kings and Carpenter of Nazareth! And no one knew in all that sleepy hollow what dreams and hopes were burning in His heart—but the devil knew when he tempted Him with kingdoms. I beg of you not to call them silent years. To me they are most eloquent and vocal. They are filled with the heroism of quiet duty. They are sublimely faithful in the least. And if you are looking for a happy Christmas, and still more for a radiant New Year, remember that, and with new faith and loyalty turn to your lowly task again.

The Influence of a Christian Home

Robert G. Lee was a native of South Carolina and a graduate of Furman University. Ordained to the ministry in 1910, he held notable pastorates in the cities of Charleston, New Orleans, and Memphis. He was president of the Baptist State Convention of Tennessee for four consecutive years and president of the Southern Baptist Convention for three consecutive years.

Dr. Lee often addressed large Bible conferences and conventions and conducted revivals throughout America. The author of several books of sermons, he was in constant demand to speak to gatherings throughout the country. He held several degrees, among them D.D., LL.D., and Litt.D.

This sermon is taken from *Glory Today for Conquest Tomorrow* (Zondervan, 1941).

Robert G. Lee

11

THE INFLUENCE OF
A CHRISTIAN HOME

As for me and my house, we will serve the Lord (Joshua 24:15).

Let them learn first to show piety at home (1 Timothy 5:4).

The Wonder of the Home

GOD MADE ADAM out of the dust of the ground and breathed into his body the breath of life. Thus Adam became a living soul. Before his Maker he stood innocent and unspotted. But with all his glory, power, and pleasure, Adam was lonely, solitary. God saw that amid all His creative works, which He pronounced good, that it was not good for man to be alone. Woman was, therefore, created—made from Adam's rib. She was brought to man—and there, in the sinless garden, they were united in holy wedlock. Upon this pure and primal pair God bestowed His divine blessing. They were commanded to found a worthy race, subdue the earth into utility, and rule the world for God. Thus God established the home as a unit of society. Centuries before there was a state, school, or church, there were homes instituted by God as places where men and women should live together in love and in happiness, where children should be born and reared. This fellowship of married love and the home which it builds is God's supreme gift to man and the safeguard of civilization. The matter of supreme importance to the nation is not the schools, not the state, not the national government, but homes which produce a noble civilization.

The home may be made in a tent, a rented house, an apartment, a mansion, a cabin. The home, as one has said, is a fold that shelters the family from the wolves of lust, strife, unbelief—a harbor in which souls anchor and abide secure from the storms of doubt and carnal stress that are without—a fortress from whose citadel the armed forces of love, truth, chastity, go forth to bless the world— a sanctuary in which faith builds an altar, opens the door of prayer, and yields life and life's destiny to God. Moreover, a Christian home is an ante-room to heaven where husband and wife "submit themselves one to another in the fear of God," where parents rear their children in God's nurture and admonition, where children obey their parents, where God's Word has a place, where the Sabbath rolls in tender blessing over the threshold—a field where love grows its orchard of most delicious fruits.

Most of what heaven is, our homes may be if we serve God and give Christ's religion the main track and not the sidetrack. A church within a church, a republic within a republic, a world within a world, a kingdom within a kingdom is spelled in four letters—h-o-m-e. If things go right there, they go right everywhere. The door-sills of homes are the foundations of the church and state. No man every gets higher than his own garret nor lower than his own cellar. The highest house of congress is the domestic circle. The rocking-chair in a Christian nursery is higher than a throne.

It is not too much to say that though George Washington commanded the forces in the United States, Mary Washington commanded George. Chrysostom's mother sharpened his pen for him and kindled unquenchable spiritual fires in his heart. If a man should start out to run seventy years in a straight line, he could not get from under the shadow of his own mantel-piece. If the modern mother throws the cares of her household into a servant's lap and spends the afternoons and nights at clubs, operas, theaters, she may clothe her children with satins and laces that would confound a French milliner, but her children are orphans. And there are too many orphans today.

Home implies a man who works, a woman who is good, a child who is taught. Only the man who works is a good citizen, for he assumes his due responsibility and his veins are the veins of blessing to any land. Only the woman who is good is fit for mothering—and the world needs mothers more than statesmen, poets, scientists, or professors. Only the child who is taught is reared to be a blessing.

Do you want to reform society? Don't mount the soapbox and give circumlocutory cycles of oratorical sonority. Go home! Don't turn columnist. Go home! No movement will move unless it moves there. No reform will work unless it originates there. No law stands unless it is favored there. No religion prospers unless it is usable there. A real democracy, after all, is a cluster of homes, not individuals.

What institution irritates the apostles of unrest? What institution disgusts the cantankerous radical? What institution confuses the wild purposes of the grouch propagandist? The home! The home is the heart of civilization. A wise teacher of the ancient world said: "Give me a single domestic grace and I will turn it into one hundred public virtues." The home is like a reservoir pouring water into every avenue in moral life, in social life, in political life, in all life. If there are not enough moral principles to make the family adhere, there will not be enough political principles to make the state adhere. The same storm that upsets the ship in which the family sails will sink the frigate of the Constitution. The door of the home is the best fortress. Household utensils are the best artillery against evil invasions.

The Home Is a Neglected Agency of God Today

This is to say that there is a damaging if not damning decline in home piety and home spirituality. There is a decline of family religion that predicts disaster among us. With the decay of our home life will come the decay of civilization. The home is where the alphabet of the gospel is first learned; and when our homes become the generators of spiritual influences, we shall witness an infusion of new power in the life of the churches. One of our great handicaps in church life today is the indifference of many homes to spiritual values.

There are evidences that the influence of the home is less strong on the constructive side than in earlier days. The home has experienced difficulty in keeping pace with alternative diversions, in consequence of which the parent-child relationship is threatened. The influence of the home is foundational and primary. So obvious is this fact that it seems unnecessary to labor the point. The defective home is the primary cause of prostitution, drunkenness, idleness, and all the evils and isms that would cause us to hand down our blood-bequeathed legacies reduced in quality and in quantity.

The purification and power of our national life is dependent upon the home. The over-production of spiritual pygmies today is traceable to the absence of great homes. Great homes are necessary to produce great men, whether that home be a cabin on the hill, a tent by the river bank, a cottage by the roadside, a mansion on the boulevard, or a farmhouse amid far-reaching acres. In Christian households is the hope of America.

We have education today, but education has not eliminated crime, even though our great educational leaders of the last century promised the abolishment of crime if only we would educate—build schools, support them, and pass compulsory attendance laws for all children. These well-intentioned men said then that in a generation crime would be a thing of the past. We did all this—but crime is still with us. On unimpeachable authority, we have the cost of crime in this country—fifteen billions of dollars—over-topping by some billions a year all the money spent for educational, religious, and charitable purposes put together. As Livy said of his day, "Our vices have risen to so great a height that we can endure neither the burden of them nor the sharpness of their remedy."

The world we live in contains all the elements of Joshua's world—the same gods beckon and the same forces prevail. The conscienceless profiteer inflames the feeling of fear and hate in the name of patriotism. The literary camp-followers of the new psychology flatter men's passions in the name of science. Self-labeled scholarship summons the Bible to appear at the bar of human reason. The hucksters of finance tease with their ballyhoo in the name of security. The alternatives again are spread before us—the inevitable option—God or Mammon, Jesus or Venus. Ultimately, like the spider, we weave the web of our destiny out of the stuff of our own being.

The Home Functions for God and Civilization When—

1. *There is Parental Authority.* Lawlessness in the nation gets its start by the fireside. The child who does not respect the authority of parents will not respect the authority of God and "the powers that be" when he comes to manhood. Many children are ruined by the overindulgence of a pair of easy-going, church-complacent parents. God said about Abraham, "For I know him, that he will command his children and his household after him, and they shall keep the way of the Lord." Today, parental authority, as some wit has said, has not disappeared, but has only changed hands. Children have taken it over, he says.

I was visiting once in a home where the little boy of the home, about six or seven years of age, insisted on picking the kitten of the house up by the tail. The kitten squirmed and squalled. The mother said, "Put the kitten down!" But he did not do so. She said: "If you don't put the kitten down, I'll switch you!" But he held onto the kitten as though it were a purse with many shining dollars in it. Then she said: "If you don't put the kitten down, the preacher will bite you!" But he didn't put the kitten down—and I didn't bite the little chap. But I left, saying to myself, "A criminal career is being started in that home."

Will Durant, famous poet and philosopher, speaking in Knoxville, Tennessee, urged the revival of parental authority as the remedy for moral decay today. He said, "All character in America has been generated in the countryside where parental authority is strong and has died in the cities where parental authority is weak. While the youth of America is faced with great problems and probably being led to the abysses and horrors of war, it is eating gold fish and reading smutty stories. Almost fifty percent of the next generation is growing up without that implantation of decency."

Recently I spoke in Chicago. While there I read from the *Chicago Tribune* a case of parental buck-passing on youths' scandals. A nasty case of juvenile immorality in the Morton High School was brought up. The high school students were involved in scandal and hell-raising. There, as is a frequent tendency everywhere, was a tendency to call the school board or the teacher to account. They forgot that the principal responsibility for the conduct of their children rest in their parents—and not with the school teachers. Judge Bicek summoned forty fathers in the Juvenile Court and charged them with this responsibility. Their sons were in trouble—some started on criminal careers. The Judge said: "Parental neglect causes ninety percent of our juvenile cases." Then he said that parents are legally responsible for civil damages caused by their children. "They might well also be placed in the dock beside children charged with criminal offenses, not to be tried for those offenses, but to be tried to ascertain whether their negligence contributed to these moral offenses."

M. L. E. Thomas, boys' secretary of the Y.M.C.A. in Memphis, Tennessee, told me of some boys who were caught stealing golf balls at the "Stop and Sock" Golf Club. The fathers and mothers of these boys called Mr. Thomas in to counsel with him as to what to do with these boys. Can you imagine the old-fashioned fathers and mothers of a generation past doing a thing like that? My old father—deacon for forty-two years in a Baptist church—would have done no such absurd thing. Nor my mother. Nor yours. Parents of years gone by would have done a little "socking and stopping" on their own account. I think we need some old-fashioned, Bible-loving, God-fearing, children-bearing, and children-ruling fathers and mothers who "command their children after them." Too many children, born of Godless parents, are more damned into the world than born into it.

2. *We must have Christian experience and influence.* Too many so-called homes are mere lunch counters with lodging quarters attached—places where children stay while the automobile is being fixed or when the movies are not running. Many children do not have a real chance

to get acquainted with their parents nor parents with their children.

Out of 120 ministers who were addressed in a western state, 100 said that Christian influence in the home had much to do with their conversion and service in the ministry. A large proportion of young people who recently joined a certain church on profession of faith made claim that the influence of their homes turned them to think on the way of salvation and eternal life. But Tom Paine said, "I was an infidel before I was five years old." And Lord Byron, marvelous poet that he was, debauchee that he was, mistreated by his mother when he was a crippled child, said, "Untrained in youth my heart to tame, my springs of life were poisoned."

Not just Sunday religion do we need, not just company religion where we are better to visitors in our homes than to loved ones with whom we live. Not just pleasant day piety, but piety for old black Friday and blue Monday, and worrisome Wednesday, and trying Tuesday, and tribulation Thursday, and Satanic Saturday. Only in this way can homes build character.

William Lyon Phelps, Bible and English teacher and great Christian, recently said, "I am extremely grateful to my parents for the religious and spiritual training they gave me. Every day of my life I am grateful. I would rather belong to the church than to any other organization, society or club. I would rather be a church member than to receive any honor in the world. The hardest task in the world is the bringing up of children, and the chief reason is that example is so much more important than precept." Can parents lie about a child's age and teach it truthfulness? Can parents receive too much change and keep that change and expect the child to be honest? Can parents tell "little white lies" and expect their children to tell the truth? Can parents refuse to pray and expect to have prayerful children? Can parents habitually absent themselves from church and expect their children to love and properly evaluate the church?

3. *There must be tongue rule in the home.* "If any man among you seem to be religious, and bridleth not his

tongue, but deceiveth his own heart, that man's religion is vain." If people do not rule their tongues in the homes, happiness lies stark dead on the hearthstone. When the husband's position as head of the household is maintained by loudness of voice, strength of arm, or fire of temper, the republic of domestic bliss has become a despotism that neither God nor man can abide. And when the wife, instead of revering her husband, is always wrangling or railing at him, it makes doleful living—makes him long for a lodge in some vast wilderness—and makes much matrimonial milk turn to clabber.

Spurgeon once said, "It must be a good thing when such women are hoarse; and it is a pity that they have not as many blisters on their tongues as they have teeth in their jaws." God save us from husbands and wives who are angels in the street, saints in the church, devils in the home. I have never tasted these bitter herbs in my own life, but I pity from my heart those who have this every day of their life. "How," Spurgeon asks, "would you like a world where all the skies hurtled with storms and all seas are storm-ridden and all mountain streams are raving mad, frothing at the mouth with mud foam, with simoons blowing among the hills—with never a lark's carol or a water fowl's splash, but only a bear's bark, a panther's scream, a wolf's howl, a boar's grunt, a mad bull's bellow?"

Spiritually dark homes make bad boys and turn bad girls into bad women. I fear that if musicians were as blundering in the musical realm as we are in showing spiritual piety in the home, what a mournful monotony of jangling disharmony our musical efforts would be! If bankers were as thoughtless in handling funds as many are in the home, they would be forced to wear clothes not found in a haberdasher's shop, and to talk to visitors through a wire screen. If doctors were as careless in their practice of medicine as many of us are in our manifestations of a Christlike spirit in the home, there would be large additions to all our cemeteries. Let us learn first to show piety at home—hourly, daily, weekly, monthly, yearly—all the time.

4. *Love must be professed and possessed.* Without love no amount of luxurious furnishings can make a happy

home. With love a one-room cabin or a two-room flat can be a home. Love is the chief luxury of any home. The real walls of the home are not made of wood or brick or stone, but of truth, love, loyalty. The real curtains of a home are not woven out of lace, but out of discretion. The real food of a home is not meat, not bread, but thoughtfulness and unselfishness. The real drink of a home is not wine, not water, not milk, but love which is both a food and an intoxicant. The real light in every home is not of electric lights by night nor of the sun by day, but of loyalty, love, courtesy—always in dear eyes shining, always in true hearts burning. The home is not a place where we are to shake fists and point critical fingers, but to bend knees in earnest prayer and to have the tongues of the just, more to be valued than choice silver.

A man's home is a real fortress in a warring world, where a woman buckles on his armor in the morning as he goes forth to the battles of the day and soothes his wounds when he comes home at night. But let us not forget that there is a vast difference in a house and a home. A house is built by human hands, but a home is built by human hearts. A house is built of such materials as carpenters use, but a home is built of invisible things of the spirit. Money buys the materials for a house, but the elements that go to make a home are priceless—far above rubies. A house may be destroyed, but no power, neither fire nor flood nor earthquake nor storms, can destroy a real home. Only one calamity can ruin a home— the death of love. When love dies, the home is in ruins—and all the material riches, successes, and pleasures of living cannot supply what has been lost. The home is more than the house. It shelters it, but love makes a house into a home and love works a miracle. Does not the house stand with sightless windows, unopened doors, hearthstone cold, spirit dead until love comes in? Yes, tables, chairs, chests, beds—are all stiff impersonal things that stand apart until two people with love in their hearts take over this house—and then these cold things warm up and become alive. Look at the dented cushion, the lighted lamp beside the table, the books on the shelves.

Listen to the sound of voices. There seems to be a sort of a breathing about them all. Love has taken charge. Only love will keep orange blossoms from turning into lemon peel. Only love that suffers long and is kind, vaunting not itself, can keep wedding bells from turning into tolling bells that announce the death of the home.

5. *We need breeding and rearing of men.* A modern poet recently put it this way:

> You talk of your grade of cattle,
> And plan for a higher strain;
> You double the food of pasture,
> You heap up measures of grain,
> You draw on the wits of the nation,
> You better the barn and the pen,
> But what are you doing, my brothers,
> To better the breed of men?

> What of your boy? Have you measured
> His needs for the growing years?
> Does your mark as his sire in his features
> Mean less than your brand in your steers?
> Thoroughbred! That is your watchword,
> For stable, for pasture, for pen;
> But what is your word for the homestead?
> Answer, you breeders of men!

6. *Christ must be given a large place in the home.* We have something of what that home would be when we study the New Testament, for Paul gives us a picture of the domestic life of Spirit-filled believers.

> Children, obey your parents in the Lord: for this is right. Honor thy father and mother; which is the first commandment with promise; that it may be well with thee, and thou mayest live long on the earth. And, ye fathers, provoke not your children to wrath: but bring them up in the nurture and admonition of the Lord (Eph. 6:1-4).

That claims the attention of all children. "Wives, submit yourselves unto your own husbands as unto the Lord" (Eph. 5:22). "Husbands, love your wives, even as Christ also loved the church, and gave himself for it" (Eph. 5:25).

"Walk in love as dear children." "Let them learn first to show piety at home."

In the home, if the mother is devoted to a life of amusement and dominated by the fashions of this world, the children conform to that pattern of character and conduct. If the father is more intent on accumulating money than on living a high and holy life, the children drink in his mammonistic spirit and imbibe his godless commercialism. On the other hand, if both parents are prayerful in spirit and exhale in their daily life the fragrance of piety, the children fall under that Christian spirit and derive their type of life from the pressure it brings to bear upon them.

Unfortunately for our country, multitudes of homes are as pagan as any found in heathen lands. Such godless homes hardly deserve the holy name of home at all. The house in which the parents and children live is little more than a place for lodging and feeding. To it they go as animals go to their shelter and their food from day to day, and of that the outcome is rank animalism in the form of human nature.

Let us not forget that the home is the unit of Christian civilization—provided it is civilizing and Christianizing in its character. But many homes are not units of civilization; they are units of paganism and forces that damage all who live with them. When will we ever learn that it is better for children to be brought up amid some physical discomforts rather than to live in an atmosphere unfriendly to faith and unfavorable to spiritual religion?

We need to get back to God's standards for a Christian home as Christ would have us to maintain it. How we need to exalt the sacredness of the marriage tie! How we need to give Christ the throne, not the footstool in our homes! How we need to offer Him the whole house instead of the attic or the cellar! We need Christlike homes where the Bible is read daily, where prayer is made daily, where love is expressed daily, where the whole family attends church together, where conversation about the things of the kingdom of God is a rule rather than an exception, where the family income is tithed and taken to

God's house, where God's law of piety and conduct is respected, where parents understand that children do not have to understand all the Bible to be saved.

What child has to know about the laws of gravitation to learn to walk? What child has to know that there are seven colors in every ray of light in order to recognize its mother's face? What child has to know the velocity of sound waves in order to know its father's voice? When will the homes cease to handicap churches by telling children that they are not old enough to trust Christ? Did the children in the wilderness when they were snake-bitten have to die because they were too young to look on the brazen serpent on the pole? Must we tamely submit to the indifference of parents and try to make a puzzle out of God's plan of salvation and thus see our boys and girls go the way to eternal doom and death? God forbid!

If many of our children were as dumb as their books at school as many parents seem to believe they are as to the plan of salvation, many children would get their high school diplomas at 40 and 50 years of age. Let us give Christ the center in all of our homes—attics, cellars, kitchens, bedrooms, closets, parlors, all. Then most of what heaven is our homes will be to the glory of God and the happiness of human families. I put on your heart what Grace Noll Crowell wrote as to our homes:

> Here Christ shall come and here He shall abide;
> Our table shall be set for our great guest—
> Our lamps be lit, our hearts be warm and wide;
> And here He shall find shelter, food, and rest.
>
> And He will talk with us beside our fire,
> And He will walk with us through every task.
> We can confide every hope and every desire,
> No question be too great or small to ask.
>
> Because He lives with us, is one of us,
> We shall take care no evil shall be heard—
> Because His ways are kind and courteous,
> We shall watch our ways in every spoken word.
>
> This is our new house. Lord, be Thou its head.
> We gladly share its simple fare with Thee.

Sit at our table, break and bless our bread—
And make us worthy of Thy company.

Thus Trusting Christ, Honoring Christ, and Serving Christ—We Shall Be Ready for the Heavenly Home.

What Mary and Martha said to Jesus, we could say concerning homes that are just houses today—"Lord, if thou hadst been here, my brother had not died." There are countless homes that have become domestic tombs built by no other cause than this—Christless hearts that walk a Christless way. Domestic skeletons over our land represent blighted and blasted homes; and these blighted and blasted homes represent husbands and wives who sincerely resolved to build and maintain a home, but later compromised on a *house*. Many young people have started out with the idea that a fine house and fine furnishings and fine social contacts and a fine bank account can assure a happy home. Journeying with this assumption, they inevitably find that fine carpets are thorny roads, that some fine social friends are fair weather friends, and that fine bank accounts have less value than they believed—and that when they have won the fine house, fine furnishings, and fine shine in the social circle, they have no home to put in their house.

They have sacrificed the things that make a home for a house. The chill of death is in the house. The fires of love have gone out. The darkness of the grave broods there. The grave clothes of the home that should have been in their house have been woven in the loom of ill temper, in the loom of selfishness, in the loom of wastefulness, in the loom of unfaithfulness, or in the loom of wrong emphasis. Often the luxury and self-indulgence which parents bestow exclude "the atmospheric pressure of godliness." Only the Lord of life can bring these dead homes back to life, the Lord who has power over death and the grave. Jesus rebuked the people of His day by asking, "Is not the life more than the food that sustains it?" "Is not the body more than the clothing that covers it?" We might justifiably ask today, "Is not the home more than the house that shelters it?"

Only as we get and have and hold the truth that Jesus should have and hold reigns in our lives and homes will we be ready for abundant entrance into the heavenly home—when the summons shall come "to join that innumerable caravan." Only in this way can we stand before Him in that solemn and glorious hour unashamed and unafraid.

Some day we must leave our earthly homes for death—whose only palace is a huge sepulcher, whose only pleasure fountains are the falling tears of the world, whose only laughter is a wail, whose only music is a sob of broken hearts—is busy. Someday, if the Lord Jesus lingers longer, you and I will have to stand face to face with the black door of death and deal with death—the one sanctity that all men respect, the one gesture that melts the hardest, the one awe that appeals to the impious, the one stroke of common sense that annihilates our folly, the one preacher of righteousness and justice and nobility whose lips cannot be stilled.

I thank God that when we are summoned to go from our earthly homes that there is a heavenly home already prepared for those who love Him and that home is the most beautiful place that the wisdom of God could conceive and the power of God could prepare. Oh, to be at home with Him! Home—with its music! Home—with beauty for our eyes! Home—with joy for our hearts! Home—with service for our hands! Home—with songs of praise for our mouths! Home—with testimony for our lips! Home—with worship for God!

Just here I am made to think of the scene set forth in the Revelation:

> After this I beheld, and, lo, a great multitude, which no man could number, of all nations, and kindreds, and people, and tongues, stood before the throne, and before the Lamb; clothed with white robes, and palms in their hands; and cried with a loud voice, saying, Salvation to our God which sitteth upon the throne, and unto the Lamb. . . . And one of the elders answered, saying unto me, What are these which are arrayed in white robes, and whence came they? And I said unto him, Sir,

thou knowest, And he said to me, These are they which came out of great tribulation, and have washed their robes, and made them white in the blood of the Lamb. Therefore are they before the throne of God, and serve him day and night in his temple: and he that sitteth on the throne shall dwell among them. They shall hunger no more, neither thirst any more; neither shall the sun light on them, nor any heat. For the Lamb which is in the midst of the throne shall feed them, and shall lead them unto the living fountains of waters; and God shall wipe away all tears from their eyes (Rev. 7:9-10, 13-17).

Let us so live that when our summons shall come to leave our earthly homes we can calmly and trustfully say what the poet said:

Adieu, sweet friends, I have waited long,
To hear the message that calls me home;
And now it comes like a low sweet song,
Of welcome over the river's foam;
And my heart shall ache and my feet shall roam—
No more, no more; I'm going home.

Home! Where no storm, where no tempest raves
In the light of the calm eternal day;
Where no willows weep over lonely graves,
And the tears from our eyelids are kissed away,
And my soul shall sigh and my feet shall roam—
No more, no more; I'm going home.

Friends will be there I have loved long ago—
And joy like a river around me will flow.

So, in thought of that day when the pierced hands that opened to us the gates of grace shall open to us the gates of glory, let us profess and possess and manifest the religion of our Lord Jesus in our earthly homes.

Before the Children Went Away

James McGinlay (1901-1958) was a gifted evangelist and Bible conference speaker whose Scottish accent and humor endeared him to congregations throughout the United States and Canada. He pastored Baptist churches in Brooklyn, NY, and London, Ontario, Canada, and published several books of sermons that demonstrate his unique homiletical style, among them *Heaven's Jewelry*, *Not Now But Afterwards*, and *The Birthday of Souls*. Dr. Herbert Lockyer, Sr., called McGinlay "a born orator" whose preaching was "unique and gospel-drenched." This sermon is taken from *Heaven's Jewelry*, which was published by W. B. Eerdmans Co. in 1946.

James McGinlay

12

BEFORE THE CHILDREN WENT AWAY

> Moreover Job continued his parable, and said, Oh that I were as in months past, as in the days when God preserved me; when his candle shined upon my head, and when by his light I walked through darkness; As I was in the days of my youth, when the secret of God was upon my tabernacle; When the Almighty was yet with me, when my children were about me (Job 29:1-5).

THERE ARE FEW biblical characters whose life story has produced more heart-warming sermons than the patriarch Job. Members of congregations all down through the ages, with a tear in their eye and a lump in their throat, have listened while the preacher related how one fell stroke of providence robbed Job of everything he had in life.

Job's earthly possessions vanished in a day; his health and strength were taken from him. A loathsome disease covered his body from head to foot with wounds and bruises and putrefying sores. As he sat upon an ash heap, scraping his boils with a piece of broken saucer, his wife prescribed as a remedy that he curse God and die. Surely all will agree that no saint of God ever tasted the bitterness of life as did that great man Job.

However, I do not believe that, for him, the zero hour of tragedy arrived until word was brought to the patriarch that his seven sons and three daughters had been carried away by death. As we come upon him in our present text, we find him indulging in doleful reverie. He is thinking in retrospect of the days that are gone, and, of course, across the horizon of his vivid recollection there steals the memory of his ten children, whom he would never see again in life. He does not say much, but up from the depths of his grief-broken heart there come words of solemn import: "Oh that I were as in months past, . . . When the Almighty was yet with me, when my children were about me."

151

It is not my purpose in this message to probe into wounds that are already closed, or to pour salt upon sores that are still open; but I feel constrained of God to speak in behalf of our children, our boys and our girls, who at the present tick of the clock are being caught in the maelstrom of iniquity, and who, unless prevented by divine interposition, will go over the precipice of sin to a Christless grave.

Obviously my remarks are pointed primarily to present or prospective parents. Let me say first of all that those children who are living under your roof are *your* children. God never gave them to the state, nor to the school, nor to the church; and none of these institutions will ever be asked to answer for them. That boy or that girl who is in your home God gave to *you*, and on the day when He makes inquisition for the blood of souls, if your children are lost, you must answer to the Lord for the trust He imposed upon you. Do you know that when you brought that little child into this world you gave life to an immortal soul that will live forever and ever and ever? Please never forget this truth, for it lends deep meaning to the rest of this message.

First, let us restate one phrase of the text in the present tense, " . . . while our children are about us," making it apply to each of us, now. In this connection, let us ask ourselves several important questions.

I. What Kind of Home Are You Providing for Your Children?

Is your home a happy place? Your children were born with potentialities for enjoying fun, and if they are deprived in their own home of this prerequisite to happiness, they may go out into the highways and the byways of iniquity, among reprobate companions, in search of the pleasure which they were denied in their parents' house. Do they joke and have a good time? If your children were put "on the spot" today, could they honestly say that the happiest place they have ever known is the home of their father and mother? Alas, it is little wonder that the teeth of some children are set on edge—they have such sour prunes for parents.

I know many a father who, in the office, in the factory, and in the shop is a "hail-fellow-well-met." He laughs and tells funny stories, and some female coworkers sigh and erroneously imagine that it must be wonderful to live under the same roof with such a jocular fellow as he. But when he returns to his home in the evening, he plants himself deep in his easy chair, gets behind his newspaper, and God help the wee boy or girl if he or she dares to disturb him! Listen, man, if you have so many laughs and jokes in your downtown repertoire, why don't you preserve some of them for display at home, "while the children are about you"?

I trust you will not think me provocative or accuse me of interfering with that which is none of my business, if I asked you this simple question: How are you and the wife getting along? Are you arguing and fighting—or being brutally polite to each other, which is just as bad? Why should your children be compelled to live in a home or grow up in a house where the father and mother are living a hell-on-earth life? Your children did not ask to be born; they had nothing to do with their birth. Listen, parents, if not for Christ's sake, if not for your own sake, if not for decency's sake, then for the sake of your dear children, won't you terminate your domestic feud at your earliest convenience? You may attend church regularly and carry thereto an oversized Bible; you may sing hymns and pray, but your piety will contribute absolutely nothing to the welfare of your children in time or in eternity, unless you can demonstrate that your relationship to God has produced for them a happy home.

It is not enough to hang upon the dining room wall the Scriptural motto, "Christ is the Head of this house, the Unseen Guest at every meal, the Silent Listener to every conversation," unless the peace and joy that characterize the presence of Christ permeate the atmosphere of your abode. If you fathers and mothers are not getting along well together, why make the children suffer? Why cause them later to look back upon their childhood days as being the most miserable of their life? "While our children are about us," let us see to it that we provide them with happy, wholesome homes.

II. What Place Does God Have in Your Home?

Do you honor the Christ of God, the Word of God, the Day of God, and the House of God? We shall never *reduce* godlessness on the street until we *produce* godliness in the home. I care not how keen you are mentally, how rich financially, or how prominent socially—the upbringing of your family is a colossal task and can never be accomplished with any degree of success without the continual help of heaven. I wonder how many of the juvenile delinquents who are burdening the taxpayers of America today were reared in homes that were happy, under the tutelage of parents who were living for God. The educators and reformers invent their schemes for the preservation of youth, but when they leave out of their plans the advice of God's Book, their instructions to child psychologists are nothing but a joke. God's Word stands: "Train up a child in the way he should go: and when he is old, he will not depart from it" (Prov. 22:6).

Do you fathers assume responsibility for the spiritual welfare of your children? Or are you numbered with those who laughingly declare, "I leave the religion in our house to the wife"? You may think that remark is funny. Listen, man, the mother of your child went down into the valley of the shadow of death to give physical life to the little one that you love. Must she now travail spiritually alone in order to keep your children out of hell? It was mother who sat up with the boy all night when he had scarlet fever, whooping cough, diphtheria, or any of the other children's diseases. Don't you think it would be nice if you assumed the leadership of your home and became the pastor of your own little flock, and each day would see to it that a chapter of God's Word is read and at the throne of God's grace a prayer is offered?

What is more gentlemanly or courageous, yea, what is more American, than for a father to say to his wife and little brood, "Shall we worship God together?" I know how difficult it is sometimes to find a convenient period in our daily schedule, but "where there is a will there is a way." Surely in the morning, at noon, or in the evening, a few moments could be found during which the family might worship God. After supper, around the table, read a chapter and then take turns in leading the household in prayer. Oh, it is thrilling to hear even the smallest child pray his little prayer to Jesus! And mind you, they will do it proudly if they see that it is not beneath their father's dignity to pray also.

You know we Scotchmen believe that the world has only known two great poets—Bobbie Burns was both of them. We hate to think that Bobbie may not be in heaven, but his life was anything but Christian; yet he knew the truth as few of his contemporaries or successors knew it. Take for example his poem. "The Cotter's Saturday Night." Nothing else more sublime was ever written. Here he beautifully pictures that humble home with the father and the mother gathering their loved ones together to worship. If you people understood the language that Adam employed when he addressed our mother Eve, I would quote a few stanzas in braid Scotch, but inasmuch as your education has been so sadly neglected, I must content myself with broken English.

> The cheerfu' supper done, wi' serious face,
> They, round the ingle, form a circle wide;
> The sire turn's o'er, wi' patriarchal grace,
> The big ha'-Bible, ance his father's pride:
> His bonnet rev'rently is laid aside,
> His lyart haffets wearing thin an' bare;
> Those strains that once did sweet in Zion glide,
> He wales a portion with judicious care;
> And "Let us worship God!" he says, with solemn air.

> The priest-like father reads the sacred page,
> How Abram was the friend of God on high;
> Or Moses bade eternal warfare wage
> With Amalek's ungracious progeny;
> Or how the royal Bard did groaning lie
> Beneath the stroke of Heaven's avenging ire;
> Or Job's pathetic plaint, and wailing cry;
> Or rapt Isaiah's wild, seraphic fire;
> Or other holy seers that tune the sacred lyre.

Perhaps the Christian volume is the theme,
How guiltless blood for guilty man was shed;
How He, who bore in heav'n the second name,
Had not on earth whereon to lay His head:
How His first followers and servants sped;
The precepts sage they wrote to many a land:
How he, who lone in Patmos banished,
Saw in the sun a mighty angel stand;
And hear great Bab'lon's doom pronounced by
Heav'n's command.

Then kneeling down, to Heaven's Eternal King,
The saint, the father, and the husband prays:
Hope "springs exulting on triumphant wing,"
That thus they all shall meet in future days:
There ever bask in uncreated rays,
No more to sigh, or shed the bitter tear,
Together hymning their Creator's praise,
In such society, yet still more dear;
While circling time moves round in an eternal sphere.

From scenes like these old Scotia's grandeur springs,
That makes her lov'd at home, rever'd abroad:
Princes and lords are but the breath of kings;
"An honest man's the noblest work of God";
And certes, in fair virtue's heav'nly road,
The cottage leaves the palace far behind;
What is a lordling's pomp? a cumbrous load,
Disguising oft the wretch of human kind,
Studied in arts of hell, in wickedness refined!

Is there a father reading these poetic lines who does
not feel within his bosom the desire to be a man such as
Burns describes? If you do not know the Lord Jesus Christ
as your Savior, why not accept Him today? Then, along
with that wife, the mother of your dear boys and girls, set
up a family altar, make your home a happy, wholesome
place to live "while your children are about."

III. Do You Reverence the
Lord's Day and Attend God's House?

Do you know that the present generation is growing up
in America during a period of great spiritual declension?

The latest statistics declare that on Sunday morning only eight percent of America's population is in attendance at a place of worship. On Sunday evening 98 percent of our population is absent. Little wonder is it that the blood of American mothers' sons has saturated seventy-two battle fields completely circling the globe. These men fought and suffered and died for the only nation on earth that started off as a Christian nation, yet it has departed so far from the ways of God, that only two out of every one hundred people living within its boundaries attend church on a Sunday night. Surely the judgment of God upon us is destined to fall. With all due respect to the political panaceas for our national ills proffered by our statesmen, we affirm that the only hope for this land that we love is a speedy return to a reverence for the Lord's Day and a wholesale attendance at the Lord's House. There is nothing more heart-thrilling than to see a father and mother walking down the aisle of a gospel-preaching church with a nice long string of lovely children behind them. It was a sad day for America when the family pew became as obsolete as the horse and buggy.

"While our children are about us," *to what sort of churches do we go?* How sad it is to think that parents will drag their children to Christ-dishonoring churches where the gospel in its purity is never preached! Such institutions, presided over by time-serving, bread-and-butter, religious politicians, are nothing more nor less than God-forsaken, ecclesiastical morgues, and constitute a menace to our land. One might as well take children to a malaria swamp and expect them to be healthy, as to rear them in a church devoid of God's blessing. If you persist in going there, you may meet lovely friends and enjoy the sociability of the flock, but you will reap some day in heartache what you are sowing today in neglect.

Go to the church of your choice, but be assured the pastor thereof is a man of God, one who is more interested in the spiritual welfare of his hearers than he is in a job. Assure yourself that the Sunday School teachers, under whose instruction your children sit, are not only born again Christians, but also consecrated to the Lord. You honor God, and God will honor you. I like that promise of the Book, "Train up a child in the way he should go: and when he is old, he will not depart from it" (Prov. 22:6). I may have trouble with my two girls and two boys, for although they look like me, they usually act like their mother! However, if we do our duty in the beginning, I am sure God will do His at the end, even although we have frequent periods of disappointment in between.

The following familiar story beautifully illustrates this truth:

> A certain godly farmer had two ungodly sons. Each morning, early, as they entered the stable to harness their horses for the field, they would find their father upon a certain spot kneeling in humble prayer. As he poured out his heart to God for the salvation of his boys, they would nudge each other and go on their sinful way. After several years of unanswered prayer, the father died. A few weeks later, on the morning of an advertised sale of the farm, the boys were tidying up the barn. With a broom, the elder of the two swept away some chaff from the floor, and there, visible before him, were two grooves implanted in the wood by the knee-caps of his departed dad. He could hear again the petition that fell from his father's lips, "O God, save my boys."
>
> The son laid aside the broom, and fitting first one knee and then the other into the hollow spaces on the floor, he knelt in deep contrition. With tears coursing down his face, he cried, "O God, for years my father prayed on this spot for my salvation. He died with a heavy heart with his prayer unanswered; but today, O God, I kneel where he knelt, and in simple faith accept the Lord Jesus Christ as my Savior." As he arose his younger brother knelt down also and after praying the publican's prayer, he also accepted his father's Christ, and together the boys rejoiced in their new-found joy.

Parents, if you have done your Christian duty and God has apparently "let you down," don't despair. It may be that your impenitent children's tears will fall upon your face in the casket and your funeral day become their spiritual birthday.

Summing up my advice, I plead with you again to rear your children in a happy, wholesome, Christian home; take them to a real Scriptural Sunday School; worship God with them in a real New Testament church. If you do this, then in the future when you look back, as Job did, to the days that are gone, you will have no regrets concerning your dear family.

Life is comparatively cruel to us all where our children are concerned. We start off as husband and wife, sitting side by each at the fireplace. Then as the babies are born our chairs grow farther apart, until at last father sits at one end and mother at the other, of a nice half moon of lovely children. But one by one they leave us, some to make their own homes on earth, others to enter their long home in heaven; and we two finish as we began, alone.

My friends, when that day comes, I am sure we shall not be talking of the money we have made, or of the honors we have won, but of the boy, the girl—our children. It may be that they have not all brought sunshine to our lives, but so long as we can say with a clear conscience that we did our Christian duty, then mixed with our sorrow there will be no remorse. Nothing could make our old age happier and our dying easier than the sweet consciousness that our children are saved by the grace of God and in love with the Christ who redeemed them. As our daughters and their husbands, or our sons with their wives, bring to our deathbed their wee children, our grandchildren, how wonderful it will be to know that the children we brought up are in turn instructing the next generation to serve the Christ we loved.

Ah, friends, whether our last illness be painful or otherwise, our going from this world will be no hardship, and when our children carry our earthly remains and lay them on the lonely hillside, within the shadow of the willows, our sleep will be much easier, because we shall know that when the day dawns and the shadows flee away, we shall meet again, never more to part.

God grant that our simple message may not only provide a hospital at the foot of the cliff for those who have gone over, but also may erect a fence around the top to keep the others safe.

KREGEL CLASSIC SERMONS Series

Classic Sermons on the Attributes of God

Classic Sermons on the Birth of Christ

Classic Sermons on Christian Service

Classic Sermons on the Cross of Christ

Classic Sermons on Faith and Doubt

Classic Sermons on Family and Home

Classic Sermons on the Names of God

Classic Sermons on Overcoming Fear

Classic Sermons on Prayer

Classic Sermons on the Prodigal Son

Classic Sermons on the Resurrection of Christ

Classic Sermons on the Second Coming and
    Other Prophetic Themes

Classic Sermons on Spiritual Warfare

Classic Sermons on Suffering

Classic Sermons on Worship